GW01239808

M
& GALLERIES
OF LONDON

An insider's guide to the
cultural capital of the world

Eve Kershman

MUSEUMS & GALLERIES OF LONDON

An insider's guide to the
cultural capital of the world

Eve Kershman

Acknowledgements

Thanks first and foremost to Abigail Willis, whose original text has been a delight to adapt and whose words have been a blueprint for the new reviews. This book would not have been possible without the help and support of the team at Metro Publications when writing this 7th edition. My editor, Edward Prendeville, has gone to a lot of trouble to save you, the reader, from tripping up on wayward grammar, and made the book into a far smoother read. I would also like to thank the numerous museum staff who have helped with my research enquiries and image sourcing, in particular:

Louise Pichel, Sean Bidder, Ashleigh Barice, George Hunt, Paulina Kulacz, Leeanne Westwood, Sarah Farrell, Bethan Wood, Ailsa Hendry, Jessica Sajovie, Juliet Smith, Colin Gale, Chloe Orji, Laura Hensser, Caitlin Collinson, Michael Hall, Ethan Beer, Monica Walker, Joanna Bolitho, Robert Davies, Kira Wainstain, Laura Gosney, Julie Bleas, Sara Chan, Charlotte New, Barry O'Reilly, Josie Spalla, The Press Office at English Heritage.

In the year it's taken to research and write this book, I have had the pleasure of visiting a great many museums and galleries in London, to experience the incredible art and history that our city has to offer. Exploring these cultural institutions has been a wonderful journey, and I have been fortunate to meet the curators, tour the exhibits, and hear their stories.

Lastly, my thanks go to all the art enthusiasts and historians for their generous support and recommendations. Without your insights and expertise, this project would not have been possible.

Contents

Dulwich Picture Gallery

interactive family days out at the Postal Museum or Imperial War Museum. There's also a wealth of weird and wonderful specialist spots, such as The Fan Museum, the London Sewing Machine Museum and the Museum of Brands. Use the handy subject index at the back of the book to track down institutions of particular interest. However, wandering from the well-known institutions to the local gems is often the most rewarding and it's these spaces that need our support more than ever like the Estorick Collection and Dennis Severs House, which continue to breathe life into their neighbourhoods.

All of these have been catalogued by area and each entry includes contact details and the nearest public transport hub, making exploring both your own backyard and uncharted territory all the easier and more enjoyable. You won't want to miss these places on your travels, and with this book as your guide, there's no excuse not to dive headfirst and get a little lost in the *Museums & Galleries of London*.

Eve Kershman

Introduction

With more galleries and museums than any other city in the world (we review 156 of them), London has rightly been called the cultural capital, not just of the UK, but globally. Wondering where to start? Then look no further – there isn't a better way to get stuck into the dizzying array of culture on offer than with this pocket-sized passport to London's museums and galleries.

While COVID19 put a strain on many of London's community spaces (and sadly spelled the end for some small museums), since then visitors have returned in great numbers to their most cherished cultural institutions. Clearly, the temporary absence of our museums and galleries has reaffirmed their importance as spaces of connection, exploration and education, as well as champions of the city's heritage.

One thing that is so special about London's cultural scene is just how much of it is free to access. For this reason in this 7th edition we've expanded our entries on commercial art galleries, to give them equal footing with major museums. Not only are they some of the most underrated institutions, but for those mindful of costs, they are also mostly free. Our national permanent collections remain free, but the cost of temporary exhibitions has risen. For this reason, each entry has been labelled either £ (5-10), ££ (11-14), £££ (15-20), ££££ (20+) or free. Forward planning helps time-strapped visitors too; increasingly it's possible to download apps and maps before you set out so you can plan your visit with military precision.

And the scope of shows on in London looks set to keep growing. Some recent eagerly anticipated openings include Queer Britain and the Quentin Blake Centre, huge renovations such as at The Hunterian (£4.6 million) and the National Portrait Gallery (£41 million), and complete rebrands like at the Museum of the Home (previously the Geffrye Museum) and the Young V&A (previously the Museum of Childhood).

London has it all – from the mammoth institutions that built its cultural reputation like The British Museum and the Tate, to fun

Central

Alison Jacques
The taste-makers of Tottenham Court Road
16-18 Berners Street, W1T 3LN • 020 7631 4720 •
www.alisonjacquesgallery.com • Tottenham Court Road LU
• Tue-Sat 11.00-17.00 • Free

Now settling into its second decade, this contemporary art gallery made its name by bringing the likes of Robert Mapplethorpe and Graham Little onto the main stage. More recently the gallery has expanded its programme to include critically important artists such as Maria Bartuszovà, Lygia Clark and Hannah Wilke.

Alison Jacques also promotes the work of younger artists like Sophie Barber, Takuro Kuwata and Erika Verzutti, helping these talents gain wider recognition, joining the ranks of Dorothea Tanning (also represented here). A visit to Alison Jacques is bound to be a rewarding experience; take a look at their website for details of their current exhibition.

Apsley House, The Wellington Collection
Home of the Iron Duke

149 Piccadilly, Hyde Park Corner, W1J 7NT • www.english-heritage.
org.uk • Hyde Park Corner LU • Check website for opening hours • £

Home of the 1st Duke of Wellington, Apsley House, No. 1 London, must be the swankiest address in town. Its plush interiors are dressed to impress, gleaming with gilt and gold to reflect their owner's status as the hero of Waterloo. With so many London museums featuring the two world wars of the 20th century, the impact of the Napoleonic Wars in the previous century is perhaps overlooked. Waterloo ended over twenty years of conflict in Europe and beyond, and when Wellington died in 1852, a million people lined the streets of London to pay their respects.

In his lifetime the 1st Duke's battlefield success brought him fame, honours and lavish gifts from grateful heads of state. Apsley House became a sort of live-in memorial to Waterloo, where high-profile guests could be entertained. The Waterloo Gallery was added for just this purpose in 1828-9, and was big enough to seat 84 people at the Duke's spectacular annual Waterloo Banquet, and to display some of the artworks given to him by the King of Spain. Among the show-stoppers are four paintings by Velázquez, including *The Waterseller of Seville* and his renowned portrait of Pope Innocent X (who looks anything but).

Other paintings to look out for are three recently reattributed works by Titian, the most important of which, the *Danaë*, hangs in the pretty Regency surrounds of the Piccadilly Room. Also here is Lawrence's stirring portrait of Wellington, looking every inch the Iron Duke. Paintings of his comrades-in-arms hang in the ultra-masculine environment of the Striped Drawing Room. Better known for his martial acumen, the Duke was also an avid music lover and the Yellow Drawing Room houses his grand piano, the earliest surviving example in the UK.

An excellent new multi-media guide helps bring the collection and its owner to life, and includes a highlights tour and an art lover's tour.

The Bank of England Museum
The museum of monetary matters
Threadneedle Street, EC2R 8AH • 020 3461 5545 •
www.bankofengland.co.uk/museum • Bank LU • Mon-Fri 10.00-
17.00 • Free

What better place to get a handle on monetary matters than at
'The Old Lady of Threadneedle Street' herself? The museum tells
the story of the Bank from its foundation as a private enterprise in
1694 to the august institution of today. Its history is a flamboyant
one – on some occasions the gatekeeper wears full 17th century
livery, and up until 1973 the Bank had its own military guard.

An introductory display in the reconstruction of Sir John
Soane's 18th century Stock Office focuses on the architectural
features of the building and shows how Soane was inspired by
classical architecture. There is also information about the room's
previous life as the main hub for the bank's customers, in the days
when it was a private company.

Displays trace the development of banking practice from
goldsmiths' receipt notes through to digital currencies, and include
one of the earliest surviving cheques (dated 8th December 1660)
and a million pound note, as well as washing machine proof polymer
banknotes. There's even a chance to handle a real gold bullion bar
– albeit one that is securely locked up in a protective case – and to
see a display of historical gold bars from the Roman period onwards.
On a more prosaic note, you can also see one of the millions of quill
pens that the bank's clerks in the 19th century got through every
year. One such clerk was Kenneth Grahame, the author of *The
Wind in the Willows*, who eventually rose to the elevated position
of company secretary. A small display celebrates his 30-year tenure
at the Bank, which included being shot at by an intruder and the
author's resignation under mysterious circumstances.

Barbican Art Gallery & The Curve
Culture in a concrete jungle

Barbican Centre, Silk Street, EC2Y 8DS • www.barbican.org.uk
• Barbican LU • Sun-Wed 10.00-18.00, Thu-Sat 10.00-20.00
• £££ (The Curve - Free) • Shop • Cafés & restaurants

The Barbican has loomed over the eastern banking district since the early 1980s. While Brutalism still divides aesthetic feelings, it has gradually won a place in the affections of Londoners. The huge complex is sometimes difficult to navigate, but there are always staff on hand to help visitors find their bearings. The building has been hugely culturally influential and was the inspiration for JG Ballard's *High Rise*, and more recently featured in Skepta's *Shutdown* music video. It is in these luscious utopian surroundings that you are primed to see some of the most interesting art on offer in the capital, overlooking the central ponds.

There are two galleries within the building that offer distinct experiences. The Curve, found on the ground floor, is a more minimalist space that takes its name from the bending and curving interior. This makes for inventive curation and for more tightly themed exhibitions which take the viewer on a journey. Recent exhibitions here include 'Our Time on Earth', an exhibition about the climate emergency and 'Claudia Andujar: the Yanomami Struggle'.

The main gallery is far more expansive and extends over two floors with various video rooms. This space is primarily where they host retrospectives, routing visitors kaleidoscopically through an artist's career. Recently Carole Schneeman and the major international sculptor and landscaper Isamu Noguchi have taken centre stage here.

On the first floor is the bar, in case (as the posters dotted everywhere wittily say) you want to 'take the edge off'. What most prefer to do is get a drink from the downstairs bar and sit by the pond. If you want to enjoy more of the building after an exhibition here, the Barbican also has three cinemas, two theatres and a concert hall, not to mention the Conservatory, which is one of the most interesting horticultural attractions in the capital.

British Museum
The first national public museum of the world
Great Russell Street, WC1B 3DG • 020 7323 8299 • www.britishmuseum.org • Russell Square LU • Daily 10.00-17.00 • Free / £££ for temporary exhibitions • Shop • Café

Established by an act of Parliament in 1753 and occupying a majestic 130-acre site in Bloomsbury, the British Museum is for many the quintessential London museum. With some 8 million artefacts and 90-odd galleries contained behind its Greek-temple-on-steroids façade, the museum is far too big a beast to do justice to in this review – or indeed in a single foot-slogging visit. Both should rather be regarded as an appetiser to a multi-course banquet.

Where to start? The Great Court is the obvious place. Transformed by a soaring roof of glass and steel designed by Foster + Partners, the British Museum's central courtyard is one of the largest covered public squares in Europe and now houses cafés and shops. The circle in the heart of this light-filled square is the Reading Room, formerly a haunt for great writers and thinkers as varied as Karl Marx, Oscar Wilde and Virginia Woolf.

For first timers, the free introductory 'Eye Opener' tours are a painless way to find your feet – each tour lasts 40 minutes but schedules vary, so check with the information desk. If you prefer to explore under your own steam, but with the benefit of some professional input, the audio app is an amazing resource, with free gallery introductions or access to special content for a modest fee, which means you can continue using it whenever you revisit. If you are visiting with children, the website also suggests 12 must-see objects for the young folk, from a statue of Ramesses the Great to a Roman pepper pot.

Highlights include the Rosetta Stone, a preserved corpse from 3,400 BC, the Elgin Marbles, the Nereid Monument – the first example of a temple tomb, the Portland Vase, a stunning example of Roman cameo work, the Hoxne Hoard and one of the more recent discoveries: the Lindow man, preserved for posterity in a peat bog from the first century AD.

If the breathless list of artefacts has you flagging, there are various watering holes to choose from. The Montague Café serves hot and cold light lunches while the ground floor Court Cafés provide a straightforward self-service experience. The posher Great Court Restaurant on the Upper Ellipse floor caters for deeper pockets and bigger appetites.

The restored King's Library, just off the Great Court, now houses the Enlightenment Gallery, a permanent exhibition devoted to discovery and learning in the 18th and early 19th centuries. This was an age of curiosity and the objects which fill this enormous room – from fossils to Easter Island ancestor figures, via classical Greek vases – tell the story of the origins of the British Museum itself, as well as the Enlightenment's urge to classify everything in sight.

The problematic nature of this curiosity, and the colonial undercurrent of much of this 'collecting' that the British Museum is part of is confronted by the museum itself. Download the 'Collecting and Empire' trail to see the museum's own take on these issues. The Sainsbury Africa Galleries show how African cultures have interacted with each other and the West. The Benin bronzes (the main site of the cultural heritage debate), ceramics, carved wooden artefacts and masks are among the attractions here with audiovisual presentations helping to show them in context. Contemporary pieces by artists such as Sokari Douglas-Camp are the focus of temporary displays.

For those looking to add to their own collections, the British Museum offers plenty of tempting goodies. A well-stocked bookshop caters for bibliophiles and there are three shops offering souvenirs and gifts at a range of price points.

The Cartoon Museum
The best of British cartoon art
63 Wells Street, W1A 3AE • 020 7580 8155 •
www.cartoonmuseum.org • Tottenham Court Road LU
• Tue-Wed, Fri-Sun 10.30-17.30, Thu 10.30-20.00 • £ • Shop

Incredibly (given that Britain invented the art form) London's first cartoon museum only opened in 2006, dedicated to showing the best of British cartoon art. The ever-growing permanent collection contains examples by all the big names, from the bitter satires of 18th-century exponents such as Hogarth to more recent works by current household names like Steve Bell. The displays cover all aspects of cartoon art, embracing not just political satire and caricature but also 'gag' cartoons, classic war cartoons, comic strips and graphic novels. Great temporary exhibitions make repeat visits here a must, such as a recent retrospective on Ralph Steadman. For those eager to sharpen their pencils and have a go themselves, the well-equipped activity room runs workshops, while the research library is available for those with more academic interests.

The Charles Dickens Museum
Dickens' last surviving London home
48 Doughty Street, WC1 2LX • 020 7405 2127 •
www.dickensmuseum.com • Russell Square LU • Wed-Sun 10.00-
17.00 • ££ • Shop • Café

The London novelist par excellence, Charles Dickens moved into this Georgian terraced house in 1837 as an up-and-coming writer; when he left two years later he was a household name. It was at 48 Doughty Street that he completed the final installments of *The Pickwick Papers* and wrote his next two bestsellers, *Nicholas Nickleby* and *Oliver Twist*, but it was also here that Dickens was overtaken by tragedy when his beloved sister-in-law, Mary Hogarth, died. An event that caused the prolific wordsmith to miss a deadline – for the first and only time in his illustrious career.

The only surviving London home of the great Victorian novelist and tireless social campaigner, 48 Doughty Street has been preserved as a museum since 1925 and contains an important collection of Dickens' manuscripts and letters, as well as rare editions. For such a literary haunt, the exhibits are surprisingly visual with book illustrations and portraits of the writer and his family by eminent Victorians, such as the gloriously named Augustus Egg. The displays also feature personal items such as desk paraphernalia and 'Dickensian relics', including a grille from the infamous Marshalsea Prison, the debtors' jail that loomed large in Dickens own life as well as his fiction.

Each room focuses on an aspect of Dickens' life – from his circle of friends to his family life, while the basement domestic quarters include a working Victorian kitchen. There's a free family trail for those visiting with children, while temporary exhibitions shed further light on topics such as 'the other woman' in Dickens' life and the unsolved mystery of Edwin Drood. If, like Oliver Twist, you're thinking "Please, Sir, I want some more", you'll be pleased to hear that they host themed events throughout the year.

The Charterhouse
650 years of London history
Charterhouse Square, EC1M 6AN • 020 3818 8873 •
www.thecharterhouse.org • Barbican LU • Tue-Sat 10.30-16.30
• Free • Shop

Originally built in 1371 as a Carthusian monastery, the Charterhouse has served many purposes over the centuries – a plague cemetery, monastery, private mansion and a charity. Each of those periods has added something to the fabric of the Charterhouse today.

In 1371 the Charterhouse was established as a monastery for the Carthusian Order on the site of a Black Death burial ground. Following the priory's dissolution in 1537, it was rebuilt to become one of the great courtyard houses of Tudor London. In 1611, Thomas Sutton purchased the property and founded a charity providing education for the young and an almshouse for the old. Today, the Charterhouse is home to a community of men known as 'Brothers'.

The Charterhouse museum offers a fascinating glimpse into over 650 years of history. There are many objects on display with some loans from institutions such as The Museum of London and the V&A. Displays start in the present day and travel back through time to give a fascinating account of the place with exhibits including the skeleton of a plague victim and a medieval plan of the site's water system. There are also stunning early 17th century Flemish tapestries, the largest of which depicts the Queen of Sheba's visit to Solomon. But the real highlight is the Great Chamber that was within the sumptuous mansion erected in 1540. It is literally fit for a queen as, prior to her coronation, it was used by Elizabeth I for meetings of her Privy Council.

Be sure to check out their daily tour of the grounds if you wish to get a deeper insight into the history that include occasional candlelit tours and vary in theme from botany to art history.

Churchill War Rooms
A World War II time capsule
Clive Steps, King Charles Street, SW1A 2AQ • www.iwm.org.uk
• Westminster LU • Daily 09.30-18.00 • ££££

Winston Churchill and his ministers spent much of World War II holed up in these underground offices, for six years a secret nerve centre for the British government and military top brass. Preserved as an historic site since 1948 and still sporting original fixtures and fittings, the war rooms are a spookily atmospheric time capsule for the years 1939-45.

Built to withstand the Nazi blitzkrieg, the war rooms have since 1984 surrendered themselves daily to armies of visitors who file past rooms where history was made: the converted broom cupboard from which Churchill telephoned Roosevelt, the Prime Minister's spartan office-cum-bedroom, the Map Room, as well as the inner sanctum of the whole complex – the Cabinet Room itself.

The on-site Churchill Museum explores the life, leadership and legacy of the man himself. Divided into five chapters, the museum begins with Churchill's finest hour – his war years – and his transformation from political outsider to against-the-odds victor. Churchill's gruelling wartime regime saw him working 17-hour days and notching up an incredible 40,000 'war miles' as he sought to keep his Allies on side. The displays reflect the multi-faceted character of their subject, allowing visitors to enjoy audio excerpts from Churchill's famous speeches as well as ponder the letter from his wife reprimanding him for his deteriorating behaviour to colleagues. Other chapters look at the rest of Churchill's life, from wayward public school boy, to intrepid reporter and army officer to maverick politician, Nobel Laureate and Cold War statesman. At the heart of the displays is a 15-metre-long touchscreen timeline that gives a day-by-day account of Churchill's life with spectacular animations for key events such as the Dambusters' Raid and Churchill's 90th birthday.

Colnaghi

Commercial gallery for Old Masters

26 Bury Street, St. James's SW1Y 6AL • 020 7491 7408 •
www.colnaghi.com • Green Park LU • Mon-Fri 10.00-18.00 • Free

Founded in 1760, Colnaghi is one of the most important commercial art galleries in the world. By the late 19th century, the gallery had established itself in Europe and the USA as the leading dealer in Old Master paintings, prints and drawings. Today, Colnaghi runs and exciting programme of exhibitions and events.

Its long history is reflected in the calibre of the works on display and its reputation for monumental exhibitions, most notably one covering the Grand Tour at the 58th Venice Biennale. Just like the renowned Renaissance works in its possession, the provenance of this institution is complicated and it actually began life in Paris as a shop called *Cabinet de Physique Experimental*. Here an Italian immigrant, Giovanni Battista Torre, sold scientific instruments and books alongside what would become the most important of items – prints. Torre's brother opened a sister store in London, which grew quickly and in 1784 Paul Colnaghi, a former employee of Torre, took over the business. Fast forward to 1826, and we see a split in the company after a disagreement between family members. Colnaghi quickly established significant connections with European museums and a fresh wave of art enthusiasts in America. Among the notable clients were prominent figures such as Isabella Stewart Gardner, Henry Clay Frick and Andrew W. Mellon. The business has since undergone many changes, but it remains a powerhouse in the art world, with a dedicated team preserving its rich legacy.

Colnaghi has two other branches, in Madrid and New York, the former owing to its specialisation in art from the Spanish-speaking world. Recent exhibitions at the time of writing include 'Barcelona - Paris 1860-1936: A Journey to Modernity', which tells the story of the two cities' avant-garde, and 'Forbidden Fruit: Female Still Life'. These fascinating exhibitions reflect the tight focus of their curation and the wealth of their collection.

David Zwirner

The Courtauld Gallery
Renowned fine art institution and gallery

Somerset House, Strand WC2R 0RN • www.courtauld.ac.uk • 020 3947 7777 • Temple LU • Daily 10.00-18.00 • ££ • Shop • Café

Comprising a series of 11 different bequests, The Courtauld is that rare creature: a display of world-class art with the intimacy of a private gallery. Its collections include those of Austrian aristocrat Count Seilern and of Samuel Courtauld, textile magnate and the founder of The Courtauld. The gallery reopened in November 2021 following the most significant modernisation project in its history.

It doesn't take long to see why the collection is so renowned. Works by early masters Bernardo Daddi, Borghese di Piero and Nicola di Maestro Antonio d'Ancona are among the gleaming gold framed treasures on display in the ground floor gallery.

The Drawings Gallery contains some of the finest 18th-century interiors in London, courtesy of Somerset House's architect, Sir William Chambers. Somerset House was once home to the Royal Academy of Art and Chambers' majestic rooms today provide atmospheric surroundings for a sequence of treasures of European art from the Renaissance onwards. Look out for Cranach's sublime take on the Adam and Eve story and an outstanding altarpiece depicting the Holy Trinity by Botticelli. Moving on to the Baroque period, the gallery boasts a stunning roll call of works by Rubens.

For many, The Courtauld's collection of Impressionist and Post-Impressionist works will be the highlight of their visit and it's difficult not to reduce this to a litany of famous names and iconic works. Van Gogh's *Self Portrait with Bandaged Ear*, Manet's enigmatic *A Bar at the Folies-Bergère* and Gauguin's *Nevermore* are a few of the highlights. The Courtauld is also home to the largest collection of Cézanne's work in Britain, including *The Card Players*, *Montagne Sainte-Victoire* and the sublime *Lac d'Annecy*.

Those in search of refreshment don't have to stray too far with the colourful Art Café on the ground floor decorated in the interior style developed and championed by the Bloomsbury Group.

Cristea Roberts Gallery
Foremost gallery for original prints
43 Pall Mall, St James's, SW1Y 5JG • 020 7439 1866 •
www.alancristea.com • Piccadilly Circus LU • Tue-Fri 11.00-17.30,
Sat 11.00-14.00 • Free

With the cluster of white cubes found in this part of town, this one is distinguished for its focus on original prints and works on paper. Hosting vibrant exhibitions since 1995, it was previously *Alan Cristea*, before the change to its current name in 2019. The gallery looks after the estates of Anni Albers, Josef Albers, Paul Rego and Tom Wesselmann, among others. Recently exhibited artists include Michael Craig-Martin, Lubaina Himid, Julian Ope and Cornelia Parker.

David Zwirner
Commercial gallery in a Georgian townhouse
24 Grafton Street, W1S 4EZ • 020 3538 3165 •
www.davidzwirner.com • Green Park LU • Tue-Sat 10.00-18.00 •
Free

In 2012, David Zwirner, which already had multiple white cubes in New York, became international, opening a London branch in an 18th century Georgian townhouse. In the heart of Mayfair, this is certainly one of the grandest commercial galleries that the capital has to offer, hosting a roster of artworks by the likes of Marlene Dumas, Dan Flavin, Kerry James Marshall, Bridget Riley and Luc Tuymans. Today, David Zwirner is an art empire with branches dotted all over the world, with recent openings in Hong Kong in 2018, Paris in 2019 and an LA space in 2023. With this in mind, it is no surprise that the calibre of the exhibitions is world-class.

The Faraday Museum
Over 200 years of scientific discovery
The Royal Institution, 21 Albemarle Street, W1S 4BS •
020 7409 2992 • www.rigb.org • Green Park LU • Mon-Fri 09.00-
17.00 • Free • Café

There's a bit of a buzz about the Royal Institution these days – not bad for a more than 220-year-old organisation worthily dedicated to engaging the general public with the latest scientific developments. And with an illustrious history, including 15 Nobel Prize winners to its name, the RI has a lot to shout about.

The museum trumpets some of the scientific greats who have worked in this building, in particular its namesake Michael Faraday, the London bookbinder turned experimental scientist whose discovery of electromagnetic induction helped shape the modern world. The lower ground floor features iconic original apparatus used by Faraday et al. including William Crooke's cathode ray tube, the gauze covered lamp with which Humphry Davy revolutionized safety in mines and prototype Dewar (Thermos) flasks. Faraday's original laboratory is still in situ but is now accompanied by a gleaming white 21st century nano-technology lab, where visitors can observe Faraday's modern counterparts at work, or perhaps just having a coffee break.

Of course, it's no good making lots of whizzy scientific discoveries if you can't tell everyone what you've done, and at the heart of the Royal Institution's dedication to communicating science is its horseshoe-shaped Lecture Theatre. This is the scene of the RI's popular science talks which started in 1800. So popular were Davy's early lectures that Albemarle Street became London's first one-way street to cope with the sheer weight of carriage traffic.

The RI has really stepped up to the mark on its mission to enlighten us about science. When London's bigger museums are packed out with holiday crowds, savvy seekers after scientific knowledge are well advised to follow in the footsteps of their Victorian forbears and head for Albemarle Street.

The Florence Nightingale Museum

Museum dedicated to the founder of modern nursing

St Thomas' Hospital, 2 Lambeth Palace Road, SE1 7EW • 020 7188 4400 • www.florence-nightingale.co.uk • Waterloo Rail/LU • Wed-Sun 10.00-17.00 • £ • Shop

A legend in her own lifetime, Florence Nightingale was much more than simply 'the lady with the lamp'. This fascinating museum follows this eminent Victorian from her privileged but unfulfilled upper-class childhood to the bloodshed of the Crimean War and the energetic campaigning for health reform that occupied the rest of her life.

Exhibits include the famous lamp, the well-stocked medicine chest that Florence took to Turkey as well as the mortal remains of her pet owl Athena, and Jimmy, the pet tortoise at Scutari Hospital. Nurses' uniforms, original letters and a Victorian amputation kit are also among the artefacts on show.

Frith Street Gallery

Contemporary commercial gallery

17-18 Golden Square, W1F 9JJ • 020 7494 1550 • www.frithstreetgallery.com • Piccadilly Circus LU • Tue-Fri 11.00-18.00, Sat 11.00-17.00 • Free • Shop

Founded by Jane Hamlyn in 1989 on Frith Street, this gallery moved to a larger purpose-built space on Golden Square in 2007. The gallery has continued to go from strength to strength with Tacita Dean, Marlene Dumas and Cornelia Parker among the big name contemporary artists represented here. Recent shows include Nancy Spero's 'Dancers & Goddesses' and John Riddy's 'Horizon'.

Athena, Florence's bad tempered pet owl, was rescued by Florence at the Acropolis, Athens, as an owlet. Named after the Greek goddess of wisdom, Athena became Florence's constant companion, sitting on her shoulder or in her pocket. When Athena died while Florence was on her way to Turkey during the Crimean War, she was very upset. "Poor little beastie, it was odd how much I loved you," she wrote.

FNM 1005.

The Florence Nightingale Museum

Foundling Museum
Museum about the first childrens' hospital
40 Brunswick Square, WC1N 1AZ • 020 7841 3600 •
www.foundlingmuseum.org.uk • Russell Square LU •
Tue-Sat 10.00-17.00, Sun 11.00-17.00 • £ • Shop

This museum tells the story of the Foundling Hospital, the UK's first children's hospital and public gallery. And what a gripping and moving tale it is, combining social injustice, creative genius and enlightened self-interest. Founded in 1739, at a time when over 1,000 babies a year were being abandoned, the hospital was the brainchild of Thomas Coram, a sea captain and philanthropist. Among the poignant exhibits are the personal tokens that mothers left along with their infants as identification. Reunions must have been rare: foundling children were renamed on arrival to mark their 'rebirth', often being given the names of famous historical figures.

The museum is also home to an incredible art collection, a legacy of the days when the Foundling Hospital was also London's first public art gallery. Under royal patronage the hospital had become a fashionable attraction and the artist William Hogarth, a Foundling Governor, spotted its potential as a venue for promoting the best in British art. He kick-started the collection in 1740 by presenting the hospital with a painting of Thomas Coram.

Other artists of the day followed Hogarth's lead, resulting in a collection that boasts paintings by Ramsay, Reynolds and Gainsborough, as well as sculpture by Roubiliac and Rysbrack. Established in an age when art was seen as a force for moral improvement, the collection was a precursor of the Royal Academy. These works by the hospital's early artist supporters are displayed in historic interiors preserved from the now demolished Foundling Hospital building.

G F Handel was another of the hospital's eminent benefactors and the composer's will and a manuscript copy of *The Messiah* are among the extensive Handel memorabilia on display. Some rather nifty 'musical chairs' allow visitors to sit and listen to extracts from Handel's works.

Gagosian
Giant among contemporary galleries
20 Grosvenor Hill, W1K 3QD • 020 7841 9960 • www.gagosian.com • King's Cross LU • Tue-Sat 10.00–18.00 • Free • Shop

The Gagosian is the great white shark of the world's commercial art galleries – sleek, grey and at the top of the food chain with its three branches across central London. Indeed, it is positively an empire and beyond the capital they have galleries across the world including, in New York, Paris, Hong Kong, and Beverly Hills.

Some visitors will have been lucky enough to see an actual shark preserved in brine, otherwise known as *The Physical Impossibility of Death in the Mind of Someone Living.* This work by Damien Hirst is arguably the most important conceptual artwork of the 21st century, and the Gagosian's 'Natural History' exhibition was the first to showcase all of the artist's formaldehyde works together. Spanning thirty years of his career, this was an exhibition for the history books.

Proof of the gallery's influence, you come here to experience the most cherished artworks that might end up hanging in some millionaire's living room, whether that be the well-established masters of the 20th century like Pablo Picasso, Willem de Kooning and Mark Rothko or contemporary genre-benders like Takashi Murakami and Rachel Whiteread. While there are only three rooms, each artwork is allowed to breathe (no pun intended) and due to their somewhat random locations, the gallerygoers are as sparsely dispersed as the works themselves.

Yes, the spaces can verge on sterile, but with free entry and jaw-dropping works on show, it is always a joy to visit one of their several London galleries. If you prefer to buy rather than spy, Gagosian have a dedicated shop in Burlington Arcade (W1J 0QJ) offering posters, books, clothing and other Gagosian related merchandise.

Other branches...
17–19 Davies Street, W1K 3DE; 6-24 Britannia Street, WC1X 9JD

The Garden Museum
Museum dedicated to the garden
St Mary-at-Lambeth, 5 Lambeth Palace Road, SE1 7LB •
020 7401 8865 • www.gardenmuseum.org.uk • Lambeth North
LU • Daily 10.00–17.00 • ££ • Shop • Café

The ancient church of St Mary-at-Lambeth, just off the busy Lambeth Bridge roundabout, might seem an unusual location for a museum dedicated to gardening. In fact there couldn't be a more fitting location, since the churchyard is home to the magnificent tomb of John Tradescant, the first great gardener and plant hunter. Since its opening in 1977 the museum has always been a refuge for the green fingered with its surrounding gardens designed by Dan Pearson and Christopher Bradley-Hole, great café and succinct display of gardenalia (gnomes and all) through the ages.

The museum has undergone quite a few changes over the years, most notably the 2017 £7.5 million redevelopment that has seen the creation of five new gallery spaces, greatly increasing the number of objects on display from the permanent collection and seamlessly combining the old church with a modern design aesthetic. One of the new galleries showcases works from the museum's art collection and space is still dedicated to the story of the Tradescants, father and son, and recreates a part of their famous 'Ark'. This cabinet of curiosities was collected by them on their travels and subsequently went on to form the basis of the Ashmolean Museum in Oxford.

Along with these permanent displays the museum runs a lively programme of temporary exhibitions that are always worth exploring, particularly when any visit can be combined with the ascent of the old church tower, offering spectacular views across the city. The new café is a real treat with great food and a view across the old courtyard garden and the grave of dear old John Tradescant.

Grant Museum of Zoology
Natural history's most shocking specimens
Rockefeller Building, 21 University Street, WC1E 6DE •
020 3108 9000 • www.ucl.ac.uk/culture/grant-museum-zoology •
Euston Square LU •Tue-Fri 13.00-17.00, Sat 11.00-17.00 • Free

Perhaps London's best-kept academic secret, you'll find the weird, wonderful and downright disturbing at UCL's Grant Museum of Zoology, with the jar of moles taking prize of place. The 68,000 specimens comprise the last London university zoological collection. On display are examples of extinct animals like dodo and quagga bones, but it's the grizzly jarred specimens and skeletons that catch eyes. Bisected primate craniums will make your head hurt, while a floating penis worm raises many unanswered questions. Another highlight is the Micrarium - a backlit cave of 2300 microscope slides showcasing the diversity of minute animal life. Free of charge and untouched by the usual queues of Kensington's Natural History Museum, go to the Grant Museum for your zoological fix instead.

The Guards Museum
Museum of regimental heritage
Wellington Barracks, Birdcage Walk, SW1E 6HQ • 020 7414 3428
• www.theguardsmuseum.com • St James's Park LU •
Mon-Fri 10.00-16.00 • £

The history of the five regiments of Her Majesty's Foot Guards – the Grenadier, Coldstream, Scots, Irish and Welsh Guards – in one smartly turned-out museum. With their distinctive scarlet tunics and bearskin caps, guards are perhaps best known for their ceremonial role in the capital but they are in fact primarily combat soldiers who played their part in Britain's military history. Uniforms include a guard's tunic worn by Edward VIII and the Grand Old Duke of York's bearskin, while among the more unusual exhibits is the wicker picnic basket used by Field Marshal Montgomery while on campaign in Italy. Guided tours of the museum are available, for groups of 10 or more at £20 a head, which in British style include tea and biscuits upon arrival.

GALAGO

INFANT LEMUR

Grant Museum of Zoology

Guildhall Art Gallery
Gallery for the City of London
Guildhall Yard, EC2V 5AE • 020 7332 3700 •
www.cityoflondon.gov.uk/guildhallartgallery • Bank LU • Daily
10.30-16.00 • Free • Shop

The Guildhall Art Gallery is home to the City of London Corporation's collection of paintings and sculpture. Its premises was designed by Richard Gilbert Scott and officially opened to the public by the Queen in 1999. In 1987 it was discovered that the building was situated on top of London's Roman amphitheatre, the extent of which is marked out in the paved area outside the Guildhall. Remains of the arena, including a section of the astonishingly intact original wooden drainage system, can be seen in situ in the basement gallery.

The main gallery focuses on the Guildhall's knock-out selection of Victorian paintings. Hung in typically dense period style, these have been arranged into themes such as Travel, Work, Love, Faith and Home and include famous Pre-Raphaelite works like Holman Hunt's *The Eve of Saint Agnes*, and Rossetti's flame-haired beauty, *La Ghirlandata*. The centrepiece of the main gallery is *The Defeat of the Floating Batteries* by John Singleton Copley, which is one of the largest paintings on display in the UK. In contrast to this rather earnest Victorian fare, a selection from the Guildhall's 1,000 strong collection of work by Sir Matthew Smith comes as a joyful respite. Smith's vivid portrait paintings are the perfect antidote to a grey day.

Returning to home ground in the Undercroft Galleries, the Guildhall's eclectic collection of London paintings captures the city in all its guises and at different points in its history. The Gallery endeavours to acquire works of art that are representative of all Londoners, and to be an art gallery about London for London. Splendid as the galleries are, they can only hold a small proportion of the whole collection but it is possible to view a good deal of the collection at the London Picture Archive website.

Hamiltons Gallery

One of the world's oldest photography gallery
13 Carlos Place, W1K 2EU • 020 7499 9493 •
www.hamiltonsgallery.com • Bond Street LU • Mon-Fri 10.00-18.00
• Free

Oozing with Hollywood glamour, this is one of the longest standing photography galleries in the world. The dark walls, black marble floors and red couches evoke a V.I.P showroom, reflecting the celebrity snapshots of its star photographer, Helmut Newton. More experimental photography is also found here, including work by Don McCullin, Daido Moriyama and Roger Ballen.

The red brick building was formerly a racquets court and music room of the Courtauld family, which makes an original site for a gallery and a welcome alternative to the purpose-built gallery spaces that are becoming prevalent in this part of town.

Handel Hendrix House

One museum dedicated to two musical geniuses
25 Brook Street, W1K 4HB • 020 7495 1685 •
www.handelhendrix.org • Bond Street LU • Wed-Sun 10.00-17.00
• ££ • Shop

George Frideric Handel lived at 25 Brook Street, from 1723 until his death in 1759 and it was here that he composed landmark works such as *Messiah* and *Zadok the Priest*. In 1968 a rather different sort of musician moved in next door at no. 23, the rock musician Jimi Hendrix with his girlfriend Kathy Etchingham. It was the only place he truly felt at home. To celebrate this extraordinary quirk of fate, Handel Hendrix House explores these two musical giants lives through careful preservation and story-telling.

'The Jimi Hendrix Experience' features the musician's recreated bedroom and living room, and a permanent exhibition tracing his life in London, which includes a replica of his *Epiphone FT79* acoustic guitar. The original was a lucky survivor of Hendrix's famously destructive approach to his instruments. There is also a documentary that gives a sense of Hendrix and his extraordinary, but tragically short, life.

Next door, Handel's Georgian bachelor pad recalls a more measured musical career. Fresh from a £3 million restoration, the basement of Handel's house is now open to the public for the first time. Entering through no. 25 is like going through a portal into the 1740s. The house recreates Handel's London with portraits of Georgian literati such as John Gay and Alexander Pope. The displays in Handel's bedroom give an intimate portrait of the man with his love of food, famously short fuse and manically creative energy that must have made him a very noisy neighbour.

But perhaps the most remarkable aspect of visiting here is the reverberating live baroque music performed in the very rooms where they were originally composed, as well as an audiovisual display about the writing of Handel's best-known work, *Messiah*. The programme is a lively mix of temporary exhibitions, baroque music master classes, lectures and concerts.

Hauser & Wirth Gallery
Child-friendly commercial gallery
23 Savile Row, W1S 2ET • 020 7287 2300 • www.hauserwirth.com
• Oxford Circus LU • Tue-Sat 10.00-18.00 • Free

Housed in a former bank in London's glitziest borough, Mayfair, Hauser & Wirth would have you mislead in thinking it held glamorous artworks, ones in which style is valued over substance. But how wrong you would be, for in this incongruous setting, many trailblazers of the art world have showcased their work. In 2010 they opened their doors with the unforgettable exhibition *Louise Bourgeois: The Fabric Work's*, which cemented their reputation. They now boast a stable of heavy-hitting artists that includes Paul McCartney, Henry Moore, and Marcel Duchamp. Not content to rest on their laurels, the gallery also own the estate of the post-minimalist sculptor Eva Hesse, making it a must-visit spot for anyone interested in her groundbreaking work.

At Hauser & Wirth you're just as likely to discover a new artist as enjoy a renowned one. Recently they've hosted the artists Günther Förg and Gary Simmons who are due greater recognition.

Unusually for a commercial gallery they cater for kids too, with their 'Family Saturday' at the beginning of each month. This allows kids and parents the opportunity to get hands-on with the current exhibition through activities like arts and crafts sessions and accessible tours of the gallery.

But the excitement doesn't stop there. In 2024, Hauser & Wirth will be expanding their reach even further with the opening of a new flagship space in Mayfair. Housed in the historic Goode Building – a Grade II* listed icon of Victorian architecture, this new space promises to be a game-changer for contemporary art in London. With their stellar stable of artists and commitment to engaging audiences of all ages, Hauser & Wirth is a gallery that's not to be missed.

Hayward Gallery
Concrete champion of contemporary art
Southbank Centre, Belvedere Road, SE1 8XX • 020 3879 9555
• www.southbankcentre.co.uk/venues/hayward-gallery
• Embankment LU • Wed-Fri & Sun 10.00-18.00, Sat 10.00-20.00 •
££ • Shop • Café

Squatting snugly in the concrete cultural complex that is the Southbank Centre, the Hayward has staged many era-defining shows since its opening in 1968, with an exhibition programme that values quality over quantity. While the nearby Tate Modern prioritises retrospectives, here they offer a unique anthology style of curation, committed to presenting engaging and inspiring art, both ticketed and free, for all to enjoy.

Its recent exhibition 'In the Black Fantastic' was one of the most raved about art shows of the year, representing 11 contemporary artists including Wangechi Mutu, Kara Walker and Nick Cave. It kaleidoscopically explored the legacy of Afrofuturism with a combination of painting, sculptures, video and virtual art reflecting the boldness of this institution. In 2023 the Hayward presented the first major survey of British installation artist Mike Nelson, which involved the use of 40 tonnes of sand to recreate his work *Triple Bluff Canyon (the woodshed)*.

From the archive, one world-class exhibition many will remember is the 2009 exhibition 'Walking in My Mind' featuring Yayoi Kusama which predated her now cult status. The exhibition also featured Jason Rhoades' *Creation Myth* that included caves collaged with pornographic images, which caused some controversy at the time.

The Hayward Gallery consists of a main exhibition space but also has the additional HENI Project Space, which is open from Wednesday through to Sunday. If you need a moment to refresh, the Hayward Gallery Café is a great place to enjoy veggie and vegan treats while taking in the view of Waterloo Bridge and scenic Southbank.

HMS Belfast
Historic warship on the Thames
The Queen's Walk, SE1 2JH • 020 7940 6300 • www.iwm.org.uk/visits/hms-belfast • London Bridge LU/Rail • Daily 10.00-18.00
• ££££ • Shop • Café

Weighing in at 11,553 tonnes, *HMS Belfast* is Europe's last big-gun warship to have seen action in World War II. Moored just upstream of Tower Bridge, she is boarded, in proper nautical style, via a gangplank. Once on board there are nine decks to explore, but be prepared for low doorways and steep ladders. An audio guide is included in the ticket price and provides the low-down on key features of the ship. For ease of orientation each visitor is given a handy map – essential as *Belfast* is a labyrinthine lady. Rather more sophisticated navigational tools can be seen on the bridge, home of the wireless office.

HMS Belfast's big guns are still very much in evidence on the upper decks, while deep below the waterline are the claustrophobic shell rooms. In service from 1939-1966, Belfast's career was eventful and displays reflect on her contribution to the D-Day landings and the sinking of the German battlecruiser *Scharnhorst*. Soundtracks are effective in bringing living quarters such as the bakery, sick bay and dentist's surgery to life, while the interactive Operations Room – the nerve centre of the ship – offers visitors the chance to run the ship through the Pony Express exercise.

To get an idea of what fighting at sea would really have been like, step inside the 'D-Day Experience', which simulates the 6-inch gun turrets sound installation depicting 05.27 on D-Day: 6 June 1944, when HMS Belfast's guns opened fire on the Normandy beaches.

In both menu and ambience, the ship's on board Stokers Café offers a functional place for refreshment while back on dry land there is a quayside café and a rooftop bar from where you can admire *HMS Belfast* and the surrounding London riverscape.

Household Cavalry Museum
Regimental military museum

Horse Guards, Whitehall, SW1A 2AX • 020 7930 3070 • www.householdcavalrymuseum.co.uk • Charing Cross LU • Check website for opening hours • £ • Shop

Set in an historic 18th-century building, this regimental museum is slap bang on the tourist trail between Westminster and Trafalgar Square. Guarded by mounted soldiers in scarlet jackets and shiny helmets, Horse Guards is still the HQ of the Household Cavalry, the soldiers who guard the monarch on ceremonial occasions in London. The museum traces the origins of the regiment from its inception by Charles II (when its members paid for the privilege of guarding the monarch) to its recent hard-core operational roles in Iraq and Afghanistan. The stable block setting means that visitors get a unique behind-the-scenes insight into daily regimental life – a clear partition allows a view (and smell) of the famous black chargers in their stalls. Videos show the rigorous training involved in getting men and horses ready for duty. Younger visitors should also enjoy the touchscreen interactive quizzes and trying on the uniforms strategically placed in the empty stalls.

Moving on, the displays look at the earlier days of the regiment and include a section devoted to its role at the battle of Waterloo. Relics from this epic confrontation include the field bugle used to call for the decisive charge of the Life Guards. A bullet-stopping French dictionary from World War I and the bridle of Sefton, the horse who was injured in the 1982 Hyde Park Bomb, are sobering mementos of more recent conflicts. Packed with a marvellous array of medals, plumed helmets, polished breastplates and swords, the displays also trace the development of the Household Cavalry into the modern, mechanised fighting force that it is today. The small gift shop offers regimental memorabilia and model soldiers for all ages.

Hunterian Museum
England's largest public display of human anatomy
38-43 Lincoln's Inn Fields, WC2A 3PE • 020 7869 6560 • www.hunterianmuseum.org • Holborn LU • Tue-Sat 10.00-17.00 • Free • Shop • Café

The Hunterian Museum is back after a six year £4.6 million refurb and it has been greatly missed. The museum displays over 2,000 anatomical preparations made by the 18th-century surgeon John Hunter. His research into bone growth, regeneration and reproduction paved the way for modern scientific surgery and his collection was purchased by the government and given to the RCS in 1799.

Glittering from its face lift, the museum traces the history of surgery from ancient times to the latest robot-assisted operations with touch screens allowing visitors to learn more about the collection and the intertwined histories of art, anatomy and surgery.

Getting lost among the cases upon cases of anatomical and pathological specimens, human and otherwise, has a certain macabre beauty. The specimen jars contain all sorts of innards and outards suspended in sepulchral solutions including the alimentary canal of a sea cucumber, a camel's palette and a collection of hernias.

After these, it's almost a relief to look at the skeletons including that of master criminal Jonathan Wild and a solitaire (an equally defunct relative of the dodo). Other human remains include the Evelyn tables, thought to be the oldest anatomical preparations in Europe and the brain of the pioneer of computing, Charles Babbage.

The Silver and Steel Gallery displays a menacing assortment of surgical instruments from East African 'thorn' needles and shark's tooth abscess openers to modern skin 'staplers' and some ingenious tools for removing foreign bodies. While the Odontological Collection displays toothsome treasures where one can compare Winston Churchill's dentures to elephant molars.

In his day Hunter would give 'peripatetic lectures' around his collection to amuse his friends; today's visitors can take advantage of free guided tours as well as downloadable audio tours of the collection.

Imperial War Museum
World's most important war museum
Lambeth Road, SE1 6HZ • 020 7416 5000 • www.iwm.org.uk •
Elephant and Castle LU • Daily 10.00-18.00 • Free • Shop • Café

War is often described as a kind of madness, so it's appropriate that a museum dedicated to 20th and 21st century conflict should be housed in the former psychiatric asylum known as Bedlam. This compelling museum takes visitors beyond merely the instruments of war to examine the impact of conflict on civilians and combatants alike.

The vast atrium, designed by Fosters + Partners, houses a host of iconic objects that act as 'witnesses to war', plunging visitors straight into the devastating business of modern warfare. A battered 13-pounder Néry Gun that was defended to the death during a German onslaught during the First World War highlights the sacrifice of war, while the mangled remains of a civilian car, blown up by a suicide bomber in Baghdad, serves as a chilling reminder of the cost of more recent conflicts.

Start with the First World War galleries on Level 0 that explores the 'war to end all wars', from escalating European rivalries to landmark battles such as the Somme, Gallipoli and the Marne, and on to the Armistice and its uneasy aftermath. As is the IWM's way, there is plenty of personal detail too, including well-preserved uniforms, poignant letters home, and battlefield souvenirs. There's a section devoted to life in the trenches, with spooky exhibits that include an armoured 'tree' observation post and a sniper's DIY camouflaged robe.

The Second World War galleries focus on the global nature of the conflict through over 1,500 carefully curated items. Among the exhibits is a piece of the wreckage from *USS Arizona* after its sinking during the attack on Pearl Harbour and the remains of a Japanese Zero fighter plane and surrendered Japanese sword. Smaller items also pack a punch such as the sick bags issued to soldiers taking part in the D-Day landings and the bedsheet diary covertly embroidered by Daisy Sage during her years interned in a Japanese prison camp.

The Holocaust Exhibition tells the harrowing story of the Nazis' persecution of the Jews and other groups before and during World War II. Among its exhibits are a funeral cart from the Warsaw Ghetto, a deportation railcar, and a huge case of items belonging to people who were killed at Auschwitz. The displays convey the remorseless scale and premeditation of the Nazi programme of industrialised murder, but never lose sight of the individuals involved, be they victim or perpetrator. Artefacts like Leibish Engelberg's prison jacket and Paul Sondhoff's toy bear ensure that the human impact of the Holocaust always stays in focus. Due to the strong content of the exhibition it is not recommended for children under 14.

With a collection of 20th-century art second only to those of the Tate, the IWM merits a visit on this count alone. The art displays on Level 3 are changed periodically, and supplemented by temporary exhibitions of contemporary art, but expect to see works by Stanley Spencer, Paul Nash, Henry Moore and Graham Sutherland. John Singer Sargent's unforgettable depiction of World War I, *Gassed*, has been allocated a room of its own. While you're on this level look out for the 'curiosities of war' that overlook the atrium, such as the mysterious metal barrel found buried in Hitler's garden.

On Level 5 the Lord Ashcroft Gallery of Victoria and George Cross Medals commemorates the 'extraordinary heroes' who have been awarded these medals and contains the world's largest collection of VCs. The displays tell the inspiring stories and outstanding bravery behind each medal and it's a humbling note on which to end a visit to a museum that explores aspects of history whose lessons still need to be heeded.

The IWM is always finding new ways to explain and give account of conflict and this continues with the opening of the new Blavatnik Art, Film and Photography Galleries in the autumn of 2023. The new gallery will occupy the third floor and explore how artists, filmmakers and photographers have sought to represent conflict and its consequences. With such development the IWM seems destined to remain one of London's major attractions.

Institute of Contemporary Arts
Mothership of radical art and culture

The Mall, SW1Y 5AH • 020 7930 3647 • www.ica.art • Charing Cross LU • Tue-Sun 12.00-21.00 • £ • Bookshop • Café & Bar

Self-described as a 'playground' for contemporary art, since 1946 the ICA has been the mothership of radical art and culture in the capital. Celebrating its 75th anniversary in 2022, its potent programme of art, literature, cinema, live music and theatre has over the years featured everyone from The Clash to Robert Mapplethorpe, Grayson Perry to Vivienne Westwood and even Tove Jannson, creator of *The Moomins*.

Considering its radical impulse, having been founded by a group of artists and poets working against the grain, it's proximity to the grandeur of Buckingham Palace only adds to the charm of this place. The building is also an interesting cross between a Georgian townhouse and a bunker, squatting as it does discreetly within its luxurious surrounds. Don't be fooled though, because entering the ICA is as close to falling down the rabbit hole as you can get. You'll be immediately bombarded with all manners of digital art.

Recently the ICA has gone back to its roots as a membership organization, with the popular blue membership costing £20 for the year. This will buy you not only the warm glow of supporting an iconic London institution but also access to unticketed exhibitions in the main galleries and theatre, the café bar, free Wi-Fi and displays in the Fox Reading Room. The full red membership gets you unlimited entry to everything on the entire ICA programme. Both blue and red membership also conveniently allow you free access to all screenings on at Cinema 3. If you haven't visited you'll understand once you do, why this is so popular and why so many choose the ICA to be a second home of sorts.

The bookshop does a nice line in trendy art mags and exclusive artists' editions and prints, while the bar and cafe offers more readily digestible fodder and is also open for evening meals.

The Jewel Tower

Remnants of the medieval Palace of Westminster
Abingdon Street, Westminster, SW1P 3JX • 020 7222 2219 •
www.english-heritage.org.uk • Westminster LU • Check website
for opening hours • £• Shop • Café

The Jewel Tower is one of the only two surviving buildings from the original medieval Palace of Westminster. King Edward III built it as a treasure house and wardrobe but its later incarnations were distinctly downmarket: junk room, kitchen, and testing centre.

Between 1580 and 1864 the tower was essentially a giant stone filing cabinet, where all the official records of the House of Lords were kept. A small selection of fascinating objects found in the Jewel Tower's moat underline the antiquity of the site and include a 9th century sword, part of the tower's original elm foundations and 11th century carved 'storytelling' stone capitals. A concise exhibition tells the story of this royal tower, those who built it, and the clerks and counters who moved in once the royals moved out.

One of the highlights of visiting here is the chance to climb to the top of the tower and enjoy the stunning views of the surrounding area. From the top of the tower, visitors can take in panoramic views of the Houses of Parliament, Westminster Abbey, and the River Thames.

But the Jewel Tower is not just impressive from the outside; the interior is just as stunning. Be sure to check out the tower's splendid 14th century ribbed vault ceiling on the ground floor, which is a masterpiece of medieval craftsmanship. The tower's intricate carvings and sturdy stone walls offer a glimpse into the past, and provide a tangible link to the history of England and its royal family.

To round the experience off there is an equally compact in-house café which sells scones, teas and sweet treats to enjoy while soaking in this glimpse into medieval England.

Dr Johnson's House
Historic house of the great man of letters
17 Gough Square, EC4A 3DE • 020 7353 3745 •
www.drjohnsonshouse.org • Chancery Lane LU • Mon, Thu-Sat
11.00-17.00 • £ • Shop

It was in the garret of this early 18th century house that Dr Samuel Johnson compiled his famous dictionary – a nine-year labour of love that resulted in the first comprehensive lexicon of the English language. The house has been restored to its condition during Johnson's 11-year occupancy (from 1748 to 1759) and retains many original features, including some heavy-duty crime prevention measures and an ingenious 'cellarette' in the dining room. Arranged over several floors, the house has no shortage of stairs, but then to quote the friendly attendant, 'the chairs are for sitting on, not gawping at'.

The house contains some unexpected treasures. A brick from the Great Wall of China is a tangible reminder of Johnson's unrealised ambition to visit it, while the garret is home to a model toy workshop presented to the house by firefighters in World War II. Changing displays and exhibitions keep things fresh for regulars while younger visitors can try on a selection of replica Georgian clothing. The courtyard outside the house contains a statue of Hodge, Johnson's much-loved cat who was, according to his master at least, "a very fine cat, a very fine cat indeed".

Johnson was renowned for his witty aphorisms, the most famous of which relates to the city in which he made his home: "When a man is tired of London, he is tired of life; for there is in London all that life can afford." Cards and collections of Johnson's sayings and bon mots are available in the small shop. Incidentally, a glance in a facsimile of his dictionary reveals that the great man defined a museum as 'a repository of learned curiosities' – a description that fits this characterful old house like a glove.

Kirkaldy's Testing Works
A celebration of Victorian engineering
99 Southwark Street, SE1 0JF • www.testingworks.org.uk •
Southwark LU • Advance booking required • £££

This unique working museum and cultural venue celebrates three generations of the Kirkaldy family who worked in Southwark from 1866-1965 testing engineering and building materials. The Kirkaldy motto, 'Facts not Opinions', is inscribed above the entrance to the firm's Victorian works building, where David Kirkaldy's original hydraulic Universal Testing Machine is still in place. Some 48 feet long and able to apply a load of over 300 tonnes, this mighty machine tested the links of Hammersmith Bridge as well as the steel used to build Sydney Harbour Bridge and parts of the Comet airliner. Lovingly restored back to working order by the museum's dedicated volunteer staff, the machine is run on special open days. The building is also home to a wide range of other testing equipment, including compression testers, impact testers, and torsion testers, as well as a collection of samples and specimens that have been tested over the years, providing a tangible link to the history of materials science.

Visit is by pre-booked tour only and midweek evening taster tours are also available. They reveal both how this extraordinary apparatus functioned and its life-saving role in developing quality-control techniques for construction materials. Other testing machines in situ include an American-made tension-compression machine, hardness testing machines and two parachute-testing machines, made by Avery and Amsler respectively.

With Borough now best known for its food market, Tate Modern and the Shard, the Kirkaldy Testing Works provide tangible (and, thanks to all that engine oil, olfactory) links back to the area's not-so-distant industrial past. The workshop and Universal Testing Machine's historical importance has been recognized with its Grade II listing. The works remain a fascinating testament to the legacy of this remarkable family and their impact on the field of engineering.

London Mithraeum Bloomberg SPACE
Reconstructed Roman temple
12 Walbrook, EC4N 8AA • www.londonmithraeum.com • Bank LU
• Tue-Sat 10.00-18.00, Sun 12.00-17.00 • Free

Right in the heart of the capital's banking district is one of the most surprising attractions – The London Mithraeum. Just 7 metres below these bustling streets, you'll find a unique glimpse into ancient Roman history. This archaeological site contains the remains of a Roman temple dedicated to the god Mithras, which was discovered during excavations in the 1950s.

The site has been beautifully restored and reimagined as a modern museum, with a stunning display of artifacts and interactive exhibits that bring the history of the temple to life. The museum experience begins with a descent down a staircase that leads visitors to a recreation of the original temple at the level of the ancient Roman city. As you descend you are given an account of how modern London has been built up over the centuries.

As visitors explore the site, they can learn about the history and beliefs of the Mithraic cult, which was popular in ancient Rome and worshipped the god Mithras as a symbol of strength and victory. The displays are engaging and informative, with interactive features that help visitors to understand the rituals and practices of the Mithraic cult.

One of the most impressive features of the Mithraeum is the way in which the site has been incorporated into the modern cityscape. The museum's architecture and design seamlessly blend the ancient ruins. Located on the ground floor you'll also find Bloomberg Space, a gallery that displays objects from the site's rich archaeological history. While it's free, pre-booking your entry slot is recommended. There is no better place to dig beneath the surface of Roman London.

London Transport Museum

Museum dedicated to London's public transport
Covent Garden Piazza, WC2E 7BB • 020 7379 6344 • www.
ltmuseum.co.uk • Covent Garden LU • Daily 10.00-18.00 • £££ •
Shop • Café

Located amid the hubbub of the Piazza, and housed in a Victorian flower market, the LTM is a must-see for train, tram and bus enthusiasts, or indeed any of the millions who travel by public transport in the capital each year. This popular museum tells the story of London's transport system from Sedan chairs to Oyster cards, and its airy iron-framed premises are populated by a colourful array of historic vehicles, memorabilia and simulators.

Lumbering horse-drawn vehicles begin the display but quickly give way to the electric and motor-powered trams and buses that revolutionised transport in the capital. Sympathetically restored but retaining a well-used feel (and smell), the vehicles are all surprisingly atmospheric and you can watch old footage of some of them in action, listen to accounts by transport workers such as 'Cast Iron Billy' and find out why posh places like Hampstead resisted the advent of trams.

The museum follows the transport story underground with Charles Pearson's pioneering Metropolitan Railway and features an 1866 steam tube train, complete with carriages you can sit in and grouchy commuters you can eavesdrop on. Misty-eyed nostalgics enjoy climbing aboard vehicles that were once an everyday part of London life, such as the much-loved old-style Routemaster bus. While the adults take a trip down memory lane, youngsters can get stuck into the numerous hands-on exhibits with no shortage of buttons to press and handles to turn. Simulators even give visitors a chance to get behind the wheel and drive a Victoria Line train.

From season ticket passes to London's 'intelligent' SCOOT traffic light system, the museum explores every conceivable aspect of London's transport network. The 'London by Design' gallery pays tribute to the geniuses behind one of the world's most famous

brands: head of London Underground Frank Pick, typographer Edward Johnston, architect Charles Holden, and Harry Beck, the draughtsman who designed London's iconic 1931 Tube map. Exhibits show how good design permeated every aspect of London's transport network, influencing everything from its artistic posters, bespoke 'Johnston' typeface and Enid Marx designed upholstery to practical details such as ticket machines and self-cleaning bus stop signs. The ethos continues today with Thomas Heatherwick's new Routemaster bus design and contemporary artists such as Tracey Emin and Gary Hume being commissioned to produce the cover for the pocket Tube maps that all of us pick up at some point on our journeys around the capital.

Although the vehicles are the main attraction, neither the social impact of public transport nor contemporary environmental concerns have been forgotten (although with a daily deposit of 1,000 tonnes of horse manure onto London's streets, things weren't too rosy in the 19th century either). A huge light-up map charts London's traffic flow live as you watch and displays flag up the challenge of climate change – a cause central to the museum's ethos with its solar tiles, low-energy lighting and natural ventilation. Recent exhibitions include 'Hidden London', an award-winning exhibition that takes visitors on a journey through the history of London's disused Tube stations, and secret subterranean locations on the Underground.

If all that travel builds up your appetite, the museum's Lower Deck café and bar provides a handy pit stop for drinks and snacks. It serves a pretty mean cocktail too – try the evocatively named Routemaster or sip a Semi-detached. For those bringing their own food, a small picnic area is provided, handily situated next to the mini vehicles of the All Aboard children's play area.

The museum's shop stocks a comprehensive selection of specialist and general transport books, collectable toy vehicles, games, stationery and any amount of items emblazoned with the Underground map and LT logo.

Marlborough
Contemporary gallery with a colourful history
6 Albemarle Street, W1S 4BY • 020 7629 5161 • www.
marlboroughgallerylondon.com • Piccadilly Circus LU • Mon-Fri
10.00-17.30, Sat 10.00-16.00 • Free

Founded in 1946, Marlborough Galleries isn't just one of London's leading contemporary art galleries; today it has global significance. But it wasn't always so. Indeed, it started from humble beginnings and when the gallery first opened it mostly sold antiquarian books, supplemented by a few Impressionist paintings. The gallery-owners Frank Lloyd and Harry Fischer were Austrian immigrants who met as soldiers in 1940. Who would've known that a mere fifty years later it would have blossomed into a trail of galleries from New York to Madrid.

For any of those that knew Frank Lloyd this was no surprise, famous for selling contemporary art for the first time to the Pope Paul VI, and convincing the Vatican to see its value (which they did, shortly afterward opening their Collection of Modern and Contemporary Art). Other buyers include Queen Elizabeth II, the Emperor of Japan and the Metropolitan Museum of Art in New York. Marlborough's impressive stable includes artists such as Gillian Ayres, Maggi Hambling and the estate of Victor Pasmore. The gallery also sells graphics by modern masters like Picasso, Francis Bacon and John Piper.

They are also well-known for investing in lesser-known artists like the late Magdalena Abakanowicz, who has just had her first (and posthumous) solo exhibition at Tate Modern. To celebrate a twenty-five year relationship with the artist they recently curated a spotlight show.

As well as shining spotlights on artists they also run thematic exhibitions from their extensive archive. In the case of the recent exhibition 'Shelf Life', curator Jessica Draper took the idea of still life and reframed it, making it fresh again.

The Museum of the Order of St John
Museum housed in a Tudor gatehouse
St John's Gate, St John's Lane, EC1M 4DA • 020 7324 4005
• www.museumstjohn.org.uk • Farringdon LU • Wed-Sat 10.00-17.00 • Free • Shop

With nearly 1000 years of history to tell, this museum has got its work cut out but its classy displays sail through. A sturdy Tudor gatehouse, one time entrance to the medieval priory of the Order of St John, is the picturesque setting for the museum, which tells the complex story of the Order from its foundation during the Crusades to its present-day incarnation as a chivalric order and founder of the St John Ambulance. Warlike defender of the faith on one hand, merciful provider for the poor and sick on the other, the original Order seems to have had something of a personality disorder. Its contradictory roles are neatly encapsulated by the three items in the opening display: a medieval sword, a pair of devotional paintings and a sculpture of the Order's patron saint, St John the Baptist.

The displays in the Order Gallery follow the changing fortunes of these warrior monks over the centuries, as they migrated around various Mediterranean strongholds. Exhibits include rare chainmail armour, ancient Crusader coins, portraits of eminent Hospitallers, silverware and furniture, as well as a gallery dedicated to the history of the St John Ambulance including a World War I ration biscuit sent back from the front. The Gatehouse and the Priory Gallery are also open to the public, along with the Cloister Garden, planted with medicinal herbs to recall the Order's caring vocation.

Guided tours take about an hour and give access to parts of the gatehouse not otherwise open to the public, such as the magnificent wood panelled Chapter Hall, the Church and Crypt. Although the Church is largely a reconstruction, the 12th century vaulted crypt is the real deal, a rare example of Norman architecture in London and the location of a memento mori effigy of the last Prior, William Weston, who is said to have died of a broken heart after Henry VIII's dissolution of the Order of St John in 1540.

Museum of Freemasonry

See behind the curtain of this fascinating fraternity
Freemasons' Hall, 60 Great Queen Street, WC2B 5AZ
• 020 7395 9257 • www.museumfreemasonry.org.uk • Covent Garden LU • Mon-Sat 10.00-17.00 • Free

While it doesn't spill the beans on funny handshakes and rolled-up trouser legs, the museum illuminates the elusive yet high profile organisation that is Freemasonry and its self-described 'beautiful system of morality'.

Located in the heart of the city, the museum is housed in the vast Freemasons' Hall, which itself is an architectural gem worth seeing. In the north gallery you'll find its permanent collection, which traces the history of Freemasonry from its origins to the present day. Here all kinds of artefacts are exhibited: from ceremonial badges made with scrap metal by prisoners of war to a 230-year-old ceremonial throne made for the Prince of Wales. If you're lucky you might even be able to take a peek into the Grand Lodge (which is still in use). While it is often in use for events, it offers an opportune chance to see behind the curtain, unveiling the landscape of this fraternity. They also have a late-night opening on the first Thursday of the month where you can experience the atmosphere whilst learning about this mysterious society under moonlight.

Freemasons' Hall is a must-see for anyone interested in the history and traditions of this fascinating fraternity. Whether you're a history buff, a fan of architecture, or simply curious about Freemasonry, this museum is sure to provide a memorable and educational experience.

The National Gallery
A mecca for fine art

Trafalgar Square, WC2N 5DN • 020 7747 2885 • www.nationalgallery.org.uk • Leicester Square LU • Sat-Thu 10.00-18.00, Fri 10.00-21.00 • Free / ££££ for temporary exhibitions • Shops • Café & Restaurant

A magnet for pigeons, protestors and New Year revellers, Trafalgar Square is also a favourite haunt of art lovers, being home to Britain's National Gallery. A top-notch permanent collection of over 2,300 paintings spanning 700 years of Western European art history (from 1260 onwards), the NG is the jewel in London's cultural crown. Some of the world's most famous paintings are housed here, among them Van Gogh's *Sunflowers*, Van Eyck's *The Arnolfini Portrait* and Leonardo da Vinci's *Virgin of the Rocks*.

The Sainsbury Wing is the striking addition to the gallery that was designed by the Robert Venturi and Denise Scott Brown and completed in 1991. The building's calm, monochrome interiors provided an ideal neutral backdrop for the glistening gold leaf and vivid pigments of early Renaissance works like the Wilton Diptych. However, the ravages of time have taken a toll on the extension and it is currently closed for refurbishment and will reopen in 2025.

In the main building, there has been some moving around caused by the temporary closure of the Sainsbury Wing with early works now integrated into the rest of the collection. The Gallery recommends that during this period of change, visitors refer to their website to find a particular work of art.

The West Wing continues to display High Renaissance and Mannerist paintings and includes works by Cranach, Bronzino, Titian and El Greco along with Michelangelo's unfinished *The Entombment* and Veronese's flamboyant set piece *The Family of Darius before Alexander.*

Baroque art dominates the North Wing, which is home to Vermeer's enigmatic *Young Woman Standing at a Virginal.* The gallery's Rembrandts are concentrated here and, looking at his self-portraits, it's hard not to be moved by the artist's searing self-analysis and his journey from cocksure, successful thirty-something to dissolute, world-weary 60 year-old. Among the works by Southern European artists, visitors can admire the curvaceous *Rokeby Venus*, Velasquez's 17th-century pin-up (and the target, in 1914, of a suffragette attack) or the darkly passionate fervour of Zurbarán's meditating St Francis.

The East Wing brings the collection into the 19th and early 20th centuries. Hugely popular, the Impressionist and Post-Impressionist galleries always seem to be crowded – among the showstoppers are a late Monet, *The Water Lily Pond*, Seurat's *Bathers at Asnières*, and Renoir's *Les Parapluies*. Escape the crush in Room 42, an intimate space hung with small *plein-air* sketches by the likes of Boudin, Corot and Degas.

Those with limited time may want to target particular areas of the collection – easily arranged if you go to the website and download a printed trail in advance. Audio guides are available for a small fee and feature a highlights tour of 80 masterpieces, but can also spoon-feed you a complete tour with commentaries on individual rooms, paintings and artists as well as on subject matter and techniques. Free, live guided tours set off daily and are supported by an excellent programme of temporary exhibitions, films, courses and lectures.

Easy on the eye, the National Gallery can be hard on the feet. Benches and squishy leather sofas offer some respite for weary art pilgrims and for hungry culture vultures the gallery has three in-house options. For a relaxed, self-service café, there is Muriel's Kitchen in the basement and also an Espresso Bar. Those seeking a substantial, sit-down meal can seek out the stunning Ochre cocktail bar and restaurant.

Thwarted artistic ambitions can be consoled in the gallery's three shops, which are abundantly stocked with postcards, mugs and exclusive gifts inspired by the works in the collection. A print on demand service means that you can take home a reproduction of any painting in the collection.

National Portrait Gallery
Gallery for people-watching
St Martin's Place, WC2H 0HE • 020 7306 0055 • www.npg.org.
uk • Charing Cross LU • Check website for opening times • Free
/ £££ for temporary exhibitions • Gift Shop & Bookshop • Café &
Restaurant

Specialising in likenesses of famous British people through
history, the National Portrait Gallery is perfect for people-
watching. With a collection of some 220,000 portraits in all
media and more celebs than *Hello!*, here at least, it would be rude
not to stare.

Following the completion of its major transformation project
'Inspiring People', which included a comprehensive redisplay of
the Collection across 40 refurbished galleries and the restoration
of its building's historic features, the Gallery reopened its doors
in 2023. With enhanced accessibility, as well as new and more
welcoming visitor spaces, the Gallery now has a new entrance –
Ross Place – situated on the North Façade.

For a chronological view of Britain's finest, take the fast-
track escalator to the third floor where the collection kicks off
with the Plantagenet and Tudor monarchs. Beautifully displayed
in an understated gallery, the works here include Holbein's
cartoon for his portrait of a bullish Henry VIII. Wall labels
explain the niceties of his family tree, dramatised by one William
Shakespeare – whose portrait by John Taylor was the first to
be acquired by the Gallery. As you work your way downstairs,
encounter a succession of monarchs and people of note from
writers to politicians.

A self-portrait by Laura Knight greets visitors who enter The
Blavatnik Wing, which houses one hundred years of portraiture
within nine galleries. Covering a momentous period in British
history, from 1840 to 1945, the floor exhibits some of the greatest
portraits in the collection and explores society and culture in the
19th and early 20th centuries. The wide range of historical sitters

to be found on this floor include Charles Darwin, Mary Seacole, the Bronte sisters, Samuel Coleridge-Taylor , Oscar Wilde and Emmeline Pankhurst.

On the first floor, a gallery dedicated to Britain 1960-1990 offers a heady mix of pop culture and politics. Stand-up comedians, fashion designers, sporting stars and models join the usual suspects from British public life pleading 'I'm a Celebrity, Get Me in Here!'

The Collection provides a gloriously voyeuristic tour through history, documenting changing attitudes and fashions more vividly than any history book. In an almost perverse reversal of the usual art gallery ethos, the celebrity of the subject holds sway over artistic merit – although, that said, there are works by big names from Kneller and Gainsborough to David Hockney and Tracey Emin.

Although photography was cold-shouldered by the gallery until the 1960s, it now features much more heavily, with examples from the 19th century, as well as in the more contemporary displays with works by photographers such as Annie Leibovitz and Gillian Wearing. Once offices, the top floor of the gallery's new Weston Wing now houses the NPG's contemporary collection – expect to see the late Queen Elizabeth II, David Beckham and Zadie Smith alongside a special gallery of sculpture busts and masks.

Late night openings on Fridays and Saturdays have proved a popular innovation at the NPG, with occasional live music and drop in drawing sessions that are archived on their website.

Located on the ground and lower floors of the Weston Wing, the gallery's café and bar are great places to relax. There is also a vaulted bar serving brunches and afternoon teas. On the fourth floor, The Portrait Restaurant by Richard Corrigan serves delicious seasonal dishes from the British Isles along with stunning views across London thrown in for free and those on a gift-buying mission can find an eclectic selection in the gallery's shop.

The Old Operating Theatre Museum & Herb Garret

Europe's oldest surviving operating theatre
9a St Thomas' Street, SE1 9RY • 020 7188 2679 • www.oldoperatingtheatre.com • London Bridge LU • Thu-Sun 10.30-17.00 • £ • Shop

A narrow spiral staircase leads you to perhaps London's most atmospheric museum. It's a precipitous climb but well worth the effort and there is a lift for those with mobility issues. The operating theatre – the oldest in Europe– is the centre of the museum and a grisly remnant of pre-anaesthetic and pre-antiseptic surgery. Built in 1822, the theatre was part of the adjoining St Thomas' Hospital but remained hidden for nearly 100 years after the hospital relocated to Lambeth, before being rediscovered in 1956. A semi-circular arena overlooked by raised tiers with leaning rails from where medical students watched the bloody proceedings, it was not called a theatre for nothing. Nearby displays of surgical knives and saws, horsehair sutures and early anaesthetic equipment leave no doubt about the horrors of 19th century surgery.

Festooned with dried herbs hanging from the eaves, the adjacent Apothecary's Garret is only marginally less gruesome. A well-stocked cabinet of medical curiosities, the Garret's small pathology collection contains some human specimens, along with some worryingly indelicate medical instruments like amputation kits and obstetrics tools with off-putting names like 'blunt hook and crochet' and 'Smellie's perforator'.

Standing as it does on the site of the original St Thomas' Hospital, the museum also has displays on medieval health care and herbal medicine, as well as nursing and patient care. The museum has also introduced very popular guided tours and mock Victorian surgery demos that can be booked via the website.

The Od Op Apothecary Shop contains an eclectic range of medical books as well as amusingly macabre knick-knacks, jewellery and herb kits inspired by the collection.

Pace London
Gallery that puts artists first
5 Hanover Square, W1S 1HQ • 020 3206 7600 • www.pacegallery.com • Oxford Circus LU • Tue-Sat 10.00-18.00 • Free

A major player on the contemporary art scene, this New York gallery's London outpost is the place to see work by some of the starriest names in the art firmament – from Alexander Calder to David Lynch. It specialises in the estates of 20th and 21st century artists.

Founded in 1960, Pace London is renowned for being an 'artist-first' gallery, working closely with the artists in their curatorial approach. Recent solo exhibitions include Kenneth Noland, Sam Gilliam, Nigel Cooke, Nina Katchadourian and Robert Nava. Its global outreach means you'll find branches in New York, LA, Seoul, Geneva and Hong Kong.

Petrie Museum of Egyptian & Sudanese Archaeology
Bloomsbury's best-kept secret
Malet Place, WC1E 6BT • 020 3108 9000• www.ucl.ac.uk/culture/petrie-museums• Euston Square LU• Tue-Fri 13.00-17.00, Sat 11.00-17.00 • Free

Voted one of London's top ten little-known museums, the Petrie is a treasure trove for Egyptophiles. With its huge collection of domestic artefacts dating from pre-dynastic times to the Roman era, it's the ideal place to get acquainted with the everyday life and death of ancient Egyptians.

Highlights of the collection include the world's earliest surviving woven garment (complete with original underarm perspiration stains) and an exceptionally fine display of Roman mummy portraits. A self-guided 'Top 10' tour and themed trails can be downloaded from the museum's website so visitors can easily track down objects relating to Ancient Egyptian food and drink, the importance of cats, and mummification.

The Photographers' Gallery
Britain's first photography gallery

16-18 Ramillies Street, W1F 7LW ● 020 7087 9300 ●
www.thephotographersgallery.org.uk ● Oxford Circus LU ● Mon-
Wed & Sat 10.00-18.00, Thu-Fri 10.00-20.00 & Sun 11.00-18.00 ●
Free / £ for temporary exhibitions ● Shop ● Café

Opened in 1971, The Photographers' Gallery was the first independent gallery in Britain devoted to photography. They exhibit all kinds of photography, with the gallery well-known for its focus on photojournalism. Their energetic exhibition programme showcases new talent, whilst retrospectives cover established names. Over the last half-century they've spent in Soho, the gallery has been one of the few places to escape becoming a restaurant or shop. The gallery remains a stalwart host of some of the most iconic photographers of our time including Sebastião Salgado, Andreas Gursky and Taryrn Simon. They also host the Deutsche Börse Photography Foundation Prize, shortlisting the best of European photographers.

In a city that is woefully absent of photography galleries The Photographers' Gallery more than makes up for this, doubling as a space for shutterbugs to congregate. Thought-provoking lectures run regularly, like a recent one on 'Digital Lethargy' and more practical ones in their Develop Workshop such as the art of 'Making the Cover', as well as artist talks with some of the best-known photographers like Martin Parr.

Their gift shop is known for having the best selection of photography books in London, and is somewhere you can easily idle an hour away. It leads onto the Print Sales Gallery where you'll find vintage, modern and contemporary prints for sale. If the prints on offer have you inspired you can even purchase cameras and rolls of film in the gift shop. Their cosy cafe is a peaceful respite from busy Oxford Street, and window seats are perfect for people-watching over a cappuccino.

The Postal Museum
Delivering fun for all ages
15-20 Phoenix Place, Clerkenwell, WC1X 0DA • 0300 0300 700 • www.postalmuseum.org • Farringdon LU • Wed-Sun 10.00-17.00 • £££

In days past stamp-collecting was commonplace, and although few of us send physical letters today, the Postal Museum breathes new life into a fast-disappearing hobby with its collection of rare examples, as well as mail coaches and vintage post boxes that characterised the postal services of antiquity. Featuring interactive exhibits, the museum is a treasure trove of insight into the people and technology that delivered our mail for centuries. Housed in a beautifully restored station, your ticket buys you unlimited access to the museum for one year from your date of visit, as well as a thrilling ride on the Mail Rail that was stationed there. The ride takes visitors on a 15-minute underground journey through the 100-year-old tunnels that once transported mail across London and showcases the ingenuity of the postal service.

Once you've been parcelled and delivered back to the museum, you'll enter their permanent collection, which holds fascinating oddities like a sheet of Penny Blacks (the world's first adhesive postage stamp), models of the now extinct post buses and even a Post Masters wardrobe to play a bit of dress up. They also have a buzzing exhibition programme that often explores taken-for-granted aspects of modernity, pulling from their archive to shed new light on topics as varied as the system of post codes and their critically acclaimed exhibition 'Wish You Were Here' on 151 years of postcards. If you want to have a more in-depth understanding of the objects on display you can download an audio guide via their app for £2.99.

The museum is complete with a play space for the little ones where they can get immersed in a mini-town with streets, buildings, trolleys, slides and chutes. A perfect family day out.

The Queen's Gallery
The royal family's art collection
Buckingham Palace, SW1A 1AA • 0303 123 7301 •
www.rct.uk • Victoria LU • Check website for opening hours • ££
• Shop

A classically inspired stone portico makes a suitably imposing entrance to this well-appointed royal gallery, which hosts changing exhibitions showcasing different aspects of the Royal Collection. Held in trust by the monarch for their successors and the nation, the Royal Collection dates from the Restoration in 1660 and includes art in every medium from paintings and works on paper to textiles. Recent shows such as 'Leonardo da Vinci: A Life in Drawing' and 'Japan: Courts and Culture', give some idea of the range of the royal holdings. The gallery's shop sells an assortment of right royal knick-knacks – from limited edition crockery to cuddly toys.

Rebecca Hossack Gallery
Gallery specialising in indigenous art
2a Conway Street, W1T 6BA • 020 7436 4899 •
www.rebeccahossack.com • Great Portland Street LU • Mon-Sat
10.00-18.00 • Free

Having just celebrated its 35th birthday, the Rebecca Hossack Gallery has long been a champion of indigenous art. It was the first gallery in Europe to display Aboriginal art and has continued to bring indigenous art to the main stage.

Nestled in Fitzrovia amongst white cube establishments, Rebecca Hossack's is unique in specialising in non-western arts. Expect to find artwork from regions as varied as Papua New Guinea, the Kalahari and tribal India. The gallery's beautiful space stretches across two floors and includes a garden tucked away to the side. Their programme includes poetry readings, academic talks, open evenings with artists, conservationists and writers and even an annual community festival that takes place in June.

Royal Academy of Arts
Britain's oldest fine art academy
Burlington House, Piccadilly, W1J 0BD ● 020 7300 8090 ● www.
royalacademy.org.uk ● Green Park LU ● Tue-Thu, Sat-Sun 10.00-
18.00, Fri 10.00-21.00 ● Free / ££ for temporary exhibitions
● Shop ● Cafés & Restaurant

Perhaps George III wasn't so mad – after all he did found this venerable institution, Britain's oldest fine arts academy, in 1768. An artist-led, independent charity with no public funding, the Royal Academy of Art is not your run-of-the-mill public art gallery. It has its own art school (whose alumni include JMW Turner, William Blake and Richard Hamilton), and offers the Friends scheme, which rewards members with access to the 19th-century Keepers' House complete with restaurant, lounge and secret garden.

The RA is also known for blockbuster exhibitions like its recent Milton Avery retrospective and shows like 'Making Modernism'. Visitors flock to the RA's annual Summer Exhibition, which, with over 1,200 exhibits, is the world's oldest and largest open submission art exhibition.

A statue of Sir Joshua Reynolds, the Academy's first president, greets visitors as they enter the courtyard of Burlington House. Although a charge applies to see the RA's loan exhibitions, works from the Collection can be seen for free in the collection gallery.

Recent exhibitions have included a look at the renowned architectural practice Herzog & de Meuron including over 400 objects illustrating their design process, architectural mock-ups and interactive displays. They also has a busy programme of events including regular talks and short courses, details of which can be seen on their website.

Whether you're enjoying the permanent collection or making a special trip for one of their major exhibitions, a visit to the Royal Academy is one of the great gallery experiences. If you need to take a break from the incredible art on show, there are a number of options within the gallery, from restaurant dining to a more relaxed café experience.

Sir John Soane's Museum
Museum dedicated to the great architect
12-13 Lincoln's Inn Fields, WC2A 3BP • 020 7405 2107 • www.
soane.org • Holborn LU • Wed-Sun 10.00-17.00 • Free • Shop

Born in 1753, the son of a bricklayer, Sir John Soane became the most original architect of his day. Luckily for us, his wonderfully idiosyncratic home he built for himself was established as a museum during his lifetime. The labyrinth of rooms, each one more fantastical than the last, is a testament to Soane's architectural vision and his dedication as a collector. Clearly, he was a stranger to our modern mania for minimalism – every available nook is home to some treasure. When they're not made of stained glass or studded with mirrors, walls are adorned with fragments of antique marble statuary.

At every turn there is something to delight, intrigue or amaze. In a particularly theatrical flourish the Picture Room is furnished with ingenious hinged screen walls that allow over 100 paintings to be displayed. Amongst the treasures here are Canaletto's *Riva degli Schiavoni* and two series of satirical paintings by Hogarth, *The Election* and *The Rake's Progress*. The walls are 'unhinged' at intervals throughout the day so visitors can see Hogarth's sagas quite literally unfold before them.

Gothic morbidity is the order of the day in the basement, where Soane conjured a melancholic monk's yard, parlour and cell, inhabited by his priestly alter-ego Padre Giovanni and featuring a skeleton in the closet. The yard is also notable for being the final resting place of Mrs Soane's terrier, whose tombstone bears the inscription 'Alas Poor Fanny'.

The Tivoli and Shakespeare Recesses on the main staircase offer a wonderfully evocative glimpse into Soane's domestic life. The Model Room is packed with architectural models of classical buildings, many of them made from cork, such as the tour-de-force recreation in miniature of the ruins of Pompeii. These rooms can only be seen by ten visitors at a time, on pre-booked guided tours as found on their website.

Sprüth Magers
Matriarchs of Mayfair
7A Grafton Street, W1S 4EJ • 020 7408 1613 • www.spruethmagers.com • Green Park LU • Tue-Sat 10.00-18.00 • Free

Spruth Magers is the brainchild of Monika Sprüth and Philomene Magers - two German gallery-owners who joined forces in 1998. Their origins are intertwined with the exceptional contemporary art scene that flourished in Cologne during the early 1980s. One of their guiding principles was to diversify the male-dominated art world and to create a platform for female artists to breakthrough. And breakthrough they did, with a star-studded roster of artists that include Rosemarie Trockel, Jenny Holzer and Cindy Sherman who have made a considerable impact on contemporary art through their innovative ideas and aesthetic vision. So too has Sprüth Mager and its ever-expanding trail of galleries, which can now be found in Berlin, LA and NYC.

Known for its enduring devotion to the artists it represents, the gallery has fostered close and cooperative relationships with museums and curators worldwide for nearly four decades. 70 artists and estates are represented by the gallery including Jimmy Holzer, Kara Walker, Thomas Demand & Louise Lawler.

Despite being in the game for over twenty years, Sprüth Magers has remained ahead of the curve and is always bringing fresh talent to the fore. It's recent exhibition 'Avatar II' was no exception in showcasing Anne Imhof's work, which took visitors twisting and turning through mazes of lockers, seemingly into the heart of the artist's psyche. As the first exhibition that covered all four of the gallery's floors, it was one of the must-see exhibitions of the season, and shows a change in the gallery towards more immersive, block-buster style shows.

Spencer House

Spencer House
Ancestral home of the Spencers
27 St James's Place, SW1A 1NR • 020 7514 1958 • www.
spencerhouse.co.uk • Green Park LU • Guided tours every Sun
10.00-16.00 • ££

This aristocratic palace was designed by John Vardy and James
'Athenian' Stuart for the 1st Earl Spencer, an 18th century ancestor of
Diana, Princess of Wales. A pioneering example of the Neo-classical
style, the house is crammed with references to ancient Greece and
Rome, transplanting details from buildings such as the latter city's
Temple of Venus. The eight State Rooms range in mood from the
quietly gracious Library to the Palm Room – a theatrical jungle of
gilded foliage symbolizing family fertility.

The 'Painted Room' is an important early Neo-classical interior
and is themed around the 'triumph of love'. Prodigious entertainers,
the Spencers welcomed the great and the good to Spencer House;
today, following a ten-year long restoration, the house has returned
to its high society splendour and, as a venue for hire, once again
fulfills its role as a social hub. For regular punters, access is by
guided tour only.

Stephen Friedman
Commercial gallery in the heart of Mayfair
25-28 Old Burlington Street, W1S 3AN • 020 7494 1434 • www.
stephenfriedman.com • Piccadilly Circus LU • Tue-Fri 10.00-18.00,
Sat 11.00-17.00 • Free

An interesting international roster of established contemporary
artists that include Yinka Shonibare, Thomas Hirschhorn, Yoshitomo
Nara, Catherine Opie and David Shrigley.

Tate Modern
A powerhouse for modern art

Bankside, SE1 9TG ● 0208 7887 8888 ● www.tate.org.uk ●
Southwark LU ● Sun-Thu 10.00-18.00, Fri-Sat 10.00-22.00 ● Free
/ £££ for temporary exhibitions ● Shop ● Cafés and Restaurant

Tate Modern is architectural recycling at its most audacious. The behemoth that was Bankside Power Station was transformed for the new millennium by Swiss architects Herzog and de Meuron into a state-of-the-art gallery for the 21st century. First-time visitors cannot fail to be impressed by the sheer scale of the operation – it's quite unlike any other gallery in London. Some 4.2 million bricks and 218 miles of cabling went into making it. To really revel in the power and the glory, go in by the west entrance where a huge ramp leads you down into the Turbine Hall. At some 500ft long and 115ft high, this is the centrepiece of the building and the setting for a succession of specially commissioned installations. Size does matter here and it has been fascinating to see how contemporary artists tackle this vast space – Kara Walker's interrogative *Fons Americanus*, Olafur Eliasson's mesmeric *The Weather Project* and Doris Salcedo's crack in the floor *Shibboleth* have been some memorable responses so far.

While Tate Britain covers British art from 1500 to the present, Tate Modern is home to the national collection of international 20th century art, as well as being a venue for contemporary art. Its permanent collection is displayed thematically, with suites of galleries being grouped together around titles such as 'Performer and Participant', 'Media Networks', and 'In the Studio'.

Displays are changed regularly but expect a challenging mix of big hitters like Picasso, Matisse, Léger, Beuys, Dubuffet, Giacometti, Pollock and Warhol, as well as more recent stars such as Cornelia Parker and Paula Rego. The permanent collection is supplemented by high-profile temporary exhibitions – recent ones have featured the work of Lubaina Himid, Maria Bartuszová and Yayoi Kusama.

Tate Modern attracts some 5 million visitors every year and even its spacious galleries and concourses can get crowded. Friday

and Saturday late-night openings are relaxed and a good way of avoiding the hordes. Except the last Friday of each month which hosts Tate Lates, offering the opportunity to party here with amazing DJs and talks. If it all gets too frenetic the Rothko room on Level 2 provides an ideal chill-out zone – its suite of maroon abstracts (originally destined for the Four Seasons Restaurant in New York) and subdued lighting are beautifully meditative, and there are plenty of benches for weary art lovers. Not all Tate Modern's rooms have such ample seating but portable viewing stools can be picked up from concourses and, given the distances you may find yourself covering, are a wise precaution.

Tate Modern's Blavatnik Building opened in 2017 (also designed by Herzog and de Meuron) and has transformed the Southbank skyline. The Tanks – originally used to store oil for Bankside power station – are the world's first gallery spaces dedicated to live art, film and installations. The Blavatnik has a viewing platform which that offers some of the best views over London although at the time of opening there was a legal battle between the tenants of the luxury flats opposite regarding a privacy appeal. If the sheer scale of Tate has you lagging, there are plenty of options including a late bar, and two new members' rooms.

As it currently stands, Tate Modern has three options for those in need of refreshment. The restaurant on Level 6 offers a seasonal menu inspired by their exhibitions and spectacular views of London, while the café on Level 1 offers a good menu and reasonable coffee. If it's just a coffee and a sandwich you're after then the Espresso bar on Level 3 may do the job. Drinking fountains can be found on Levels 0, 2, 3, and 4 and there is a picnic area for family use.

For those planning a double dose of Tate, a fast boat service runs between Tate Britain and Tate Modern capitalising on both venues' riverside locations.

The Tower of London
The grandest palace and most gruesome prison
Tower Hill, EC3N 4AB • 0844 482 7777 • www.hrp.org.uk •
Tower Hill LU • Daily 09.00-17.30 • £££ • Shops • Cafés &
Restaurant

London's tourist trail wouldn't be complete without the Tower.
Rich in tradition, history and the special brand of arcane ceremony
that Britain does so well, the Tower attracts visitors in their millions,
despite the hefty entrance prices. The traditional guardians of the
Tower, the Beefeaters, double up as guides and lead regular free
tours and talks, giving plenty of coverage to the Tower's bloodier
interludes. For those going it alone, the buildings are well-labelled
and free maps can be downloaded in advance from the website;
alternatively hire an audio tour for a small extra charge. Visitors
with small children should note that access to many of the towers
is via narrow staircases, so push chairs must be left outside.

Built as a palace by William the Conqueror, the Tower has
in its time also served as a royal arsenal, menagerie, torture
chamber, mint and jewel house. The luxurious medieval quarters
enjoyed by Henry III and his son Edward I have been painstakingly
recreated but the Tower is perhaps best known as a royal prison,
and several of its walls still bear the inscriptions carved by 'guests'
– the astrological clock engraved in the Salt Tower by suspected
sorcerer Hugh Draper is a notably elaborate variation on the 'I woz
'ere' school of graffiti. Other notable guests include Sir Walter
Raleigh, who after 13 years a prisoner made himself very much at
home and even grew his own tobacco, as well as blatant criminals
like Hitler's Deputy Führer, Rudolf Hess and even the Kray Twins.
The site where two of King Henry VIII's wives got the chop is
commemorated with a plaque.

Metalwork of a different kind can be admired in the Jewel
House where the coronation regalia of British monarchs make for
a dazzling display. The Cullinan diamond is the world's largest top-
quality cut diamond while older regalia include the St Edward's
Crown and the 12th century Coronation spoon.

Two Temple Place
Neo-Gothic mansion turned exhibition space
2 Temple Place, WC2R 3BD • 020 7836 3715 • www.
twotempleplace.org • Temple LU • Tue, Thu-Sat 11:00-18:00,
Wed 11:00-21:00, Sun 11:00-16:30 • £ • Shop • Café

It's rare for a gallery to meet all the criteria, but Two Temple Place passes with flying colors. Not only does it boast a fascinating history and an opulently gorgeous setting, but it's also home to some of the most exciting exhibitions in the capital. Opening its doors in 2011, it's a wonder how this neo-Gothic mansion wasn't turned into a gallery sooner. With its intricate woodwork and stained-glass windows, the location is just as likely to leave you inspired as the art within it.

Designed by John Loughborough in 1895 for William Waldorf Astor, an American-British aristocrat, the building is full of interesting details. Once described as "Victoriana meets Disney," it features a weather vane that represents the caravel Santa Maria, on which Columbus sailed to America, symbolizing the connection of the path of discovery of his ancestor John Jacob Astor, who with his various nefarious trade ventures was one of the richest people in modern history. The rooms combine lavish and ornate elements, with expensive materials like marble and mahogany used in their construction. However, the decor also includes unusual and eclectic touches, such as the characters from The Three Musketeers on the banisters of the main staircase and the gilded frieze in the Great Hall featuring a mix of historical and fictional figures, including Pocahontas, Machiavelli and Marie Antoinette.

In contrast to the colonial history of the building, the gallery today presents exhibitions with a global and political nature. Its recent exhibition 'State-less' explored photography and digital works from contemporary Southeast Asian artists, while its critically acclaimed show 'Body Vessel Clay' highlighted the work of black female potters. A real hidden gem.

The Wallace Collection
Art collection of the Hertford family
Hertford House, Manchester Square, W1U 3BN • 020 7563 9500
• www.wallacecollection.org • Bond Street LU • Daily 10.00-17.00
• Free / ££ for temporary exhibitions • Shop • Restaurant

Bequeathed to the nation in 1897 and housed in a sumptuous Italianate palazzo in a leafy Marylebone square, it's chock-full of fine and decorative artworks acquired in the 18th and 19th centuries by the aristocratic and scandalous Hertford family. Its 25 galleries are a cornucopia for connoisseurs, but the casual visitor will enjoy the collection's ambience as much its artefacts. It has an old-fashioned aura of discreet luxury, with antique clocks ticking quietly in gracious rooms, and friendly, helpful room stewards.

Many famous paintings reside here – Frans Hals' *The Laughing Cavalier*, Poussin's *A Dance to the Music of Time* and Fragonard's deliciously frothy *The Swing* among them. Some of the subject matter is on the racy side – there's a wonderfully louche portrait of Nelson's squeeze Lady Hamilton, reclining on a leopard skin in a state of semi-undress, as well as a clutch of risqué Dutch genre paintings like Jan Steyn's *The Lute Player*.

Clearly, the Hertford family had an appetite for the good things in life, and an ongoing refurbishment programme is bringing the sumptuous interiors of the Wallace back up to the mark. The Great Gallery – described by art historian Kenneth Clark as 'the greatest picture gallery in Europe' –holds masterpieces by the likes of Titian, Murillo, Reubens, Reynolds and Velasquez.

For a small fee audio tours help the visitor make the most of this diversity, and there is a multimedia guide for children. Free hour-long highlight tours are held daily 14.30–15.30.

Visitor facilities here are in keeping with the high-end surroundings – the Marquesses of Hertford didn't slum it and neither will you. The airy, glass-roofed courtyard of Hertford House is home to a popular brasserie style restaurant (lunch booking is advised).

White Cube
Best of contemporary art
25-26 Mason's Yard, St James's, SW1Y 6BU • Piccadilly Circus LU • 020 7766 3550 • www.whitecube.com • Tue-Sat 10.00-18.00 • Free

So cutting-edge it hurts, White Cube is the *ne plus ultra* of galleries dealing in contemporary art. The sleek purpose-built gallery in Mason's Yard opened in 2006 and houses two gallery spaces. While famous for representing British contemporary artists like Damien Hirst, Gilbert & George and Tracy Emin, they have recently branched out to represent non-western artists. This makes it a gallery full of surprises, as with their recent exhibition *Diario de Plantas* that platformed Gabriel Orozco, a Mexican artist who lives between Tokyo and Mexico City and whose ink blot flowers are a beautiful reflection on fragile ecologies.

Given how tucked away the gallery is, you'll likely have the space to yourself – the perfect environment to absorb the art as well as providing a stillness rare to find in this busy part of town. Free entry, a great pedestrian thoroughfare, and in the heart of London's contemporary art scene – be sure to peg White Cube on any itinerary for the area.

180 Studios, 180 The Strand
Subterranean digital art venue
180 Strand, WC2R 1EA • www.180thestrand.com • Temple LU •
Sat-Sun 10.00-18.00 & Fri 10.00-19.00 • £

In its short time since opening in 2016, 180 The Strand has been a welcome addition to London's art scene with a host of immersive exhibitions on digital art.

Its cavernous brutalist space lends itself well to this genre of art - with its neon palettes and mind-bending visuals that border on being epilepsy-inducing. Their most recent exhibition 'Future Shock' was quintessentially 180 the Strand – featuring Ryoji Ikeda and Ibby Njoya among others, it imagined futures evoked a cyberpunk alternate reality with a maze of short films, optical illusions and light shows.

The gallery is also home to a cinema, and it has even hosted exhibitions on various Wes Anderson films including *Isle of Dogs* and most recently *The French Dispatch*, complete with real props, artwork, miniatures, and costumes, which culminated in a working recreation of the film's cafe, *Le Sans Blague*. So if you'd ever wanted to live out your not-so-accidentally-Wes-Anderson fantasy then we imagine there will be another such exhibition on the horizon, allowing the visitor to step into his films.

Their screening of *Broken Spectre* with Richard Mosse was so popular it was extended by an extra six months, alongside his photography that explored the corrosive climate destruction of the Amazon rainforest. The political nature of much of the artwork on show absorbs differently in this subterranean enclave, like going in a sensory deprivation tank, the noise and chaos of the surrounding West End feel eerily distant.

More than any other the boundaries between physical and virtual are bent in this space so give yourself a moment to readjust to regal central London before exiting via the Strand.

North

Ben Uri Gallery & Museum

Europe's only gallery for émigré artists
108a Boundary Road, NW8 0RH ● 020 7604 3991 ●
www.benuri.org ● South Hampstead LO ● Check website for
opening hours ● Free

Ben Uri was founded in 1915 in Whitechapel, East London, to provide a cultural home for Jewish artists who were treated as outsiders by the establishment. Its renowned collection contains some 900 works by artists from 40 countries of birth. Originally primarily from the Jewish diaspora including world-class examples by Chagall, Soutine, Auerbach, Bomberg and Kossoff these works sit alongside fine examples by the wider immigrant community including Nasser Azam (Pakistan) Lancelot Ribeiro (Indian) and Benedict Enwonwu (Nigerian).

In 2018, Ben Uri turned the traditional museum model upside down and became a digital institution enhanced by its physical presence. Benuri.org, alongside benuricollection.org.uk and buru.org.uk lead the way in creating digital content reflecting both the immigrant focus of the museum and the physical presentations of collection, library, and exhibitions.

Ben Uri moved to its current smaller premises in 2002. There it has made a virtue out of a necessity by curating small scale but dazzling exhibitions supported by its extensive art library.

The British Library

A base for Britain's bibliophiles

96 Euston Road, NW1 2DB • 020 7412 7332 • www.bl.uk
• Euston LU • Mon-Thu 09.30-20.00, Fri 09.30-18.00, Sat 09.30-17.00, Sun 11.00-17.00• £ • Shop • Café & Restaurant

Condemned in some quarters as 'one of the ugliest buildings in the world' when it opened in 1998, the British Library building, designed by Colin St John Wilson, has gone on to become a much-loved London landmark.

'Treasures of the British Library', the permanent exhibition in The John Ritblat Gallery, is a bibliographic tour de force. With books and manuscripts spanning some 3000 years, this is the place to pore over historic documents like Magna Carta, Shakespeare's *First Folio* or Captain Scott's last polar diary. Early maps offer insights into our ancestors' view of the world and there is a copious selection of sacred texts such as the *Golden Haggadah* and the *Luttrell Psaltar*. The Literature section includes some rare manuscripts, Lewis Carroll's meticulously handwritten copy of *Alice in Wonderland* and James Joyce's manuscript of *Finnegans Wake* among them. A Leonardo da Vinci notebook, written in his signature 'mirror writing', is one of the gems in the small Science section while over in Music, Beatles' pop songs share the limelight with Handel's *Messiah*.

Unsurprisingly, given the priceless nature of the exhibits, the lighting is low and items are kept safely behind glass. Ingeniously interactive, 'Turning the Pages' gets around the restrictions of display – its touchscreen computers let you leaf through four of the library's most distinguished manuscripts at your leisure.

If you are more stamp collector than bookworm, head for the upper ground floor to find the Philatelic Exhibition. Showcasing around 80,000 stamps (a fraction of the library's total holding), the displays are organised by collection and theme, and contain some rare examples. A programme of special exhibitions in the PACCAR Gallery complements the permanent displays; recent shows have included an exhibition about the British Chinese Community.

Burgh House
Historic house in the heart of Hampstead

Burgh House, New End Square, NW3 1LT • 020 7431 0144 • www.
burghhouse.org.uk • Hampstead LU • Wed-Fri & Sun 10.00-16.00 •
Free • Shop • Café

Located just off Hampstead's bustling high street, the charming
Burgh House museum is a great starting point for anyone exploring
this area of London. The Grade I listed Queen Anne house was built
in 1704 and served as a private residence for most of its existence,
with notable occupants including Whig politician Nathaniel Booth
(who lived there from 1743 to 1759), Reverend Allatson Burgh
(1822-1856), from whom the house takes its name, and George
Bambridge, husband of Rudyard Kipling's daughter Elsie. After the
house was left unoccupied in 1937, it gradually fell into disrepair
until a group of local residents rescued it in 1979. The newly-formed
charity, the Burgh House Trust, eventually took over the lease of the
building and transformed it into a space for the local community.

Today, Burgh House is a dynamic hub for art, events, and
history. Visitors can explore the rich heritage of Hampstead and
enjoy a diverse programme of cultural events, including exhibitions,
talks, concerts, and workshops. The museum boasts a fascinating
collection of objects related to the history of the house, the local
area, and its extraordinary former residents. The collection began
as an amateur museum created by Christopher and Diana Wade in
1979 and has since grown to include nearly 5,000 objects.

One particularly noteworthy feature of the house is the
exquisitely crafted staircase, with its barley-twist balusters and
fluted columns adorned with elaborate pilasters marking each turn.
Visitors can also head down to the basement to enjoy delicious
home-cooked food at the excellent café.

Camden Art Centre
Contemporary art for the community
Arkwright Road, NW3 6DG ● 020 7472 5500 ● www.
camdenartcentre.org ● Finchley Road LU ● Tue-Sun 11.00-18.00,
Thu 11.00-21.00 ● Free ● Shop ● Café

This respected contemporary art venue celebrated its 50th year in 2015. Housed in a former library, the centre's facilities were totally upgraded in 2004 and include gallery space, artists' studios, a lovely café, and a garden where you can dine al fresco or just listen to the birds. What hasn't changed over the years is the centre's inspirational 'roll up your sleeves and get stuck in' approach to the visual arts, with visitors being encouraged to get involved in the integrated programme of exhibitions, educational projects and courses, artist-led workshops, exhibition tours and talks.

The centre maintains its policy of showing both established and emerging artists and past exhibitions have showcased the German-Swiss artist Dieter Roth, installation art pioneer Sheelagh Wakely, and film-maker Ben Rivers. A rolling programme of artist residencies is an added draw – with regular 'open studio' slots allowing the public to see work in progress.

Estorick Collection of Modern Italian Art
Italian art gallery in the heart of Islington
Northampton Lodge, 39a Canonbury Square, N1 2AN •
020 7704 9522 • www.estorickcollection.com • Highbury and
Islington LU • Check website for opening hours • £ • Shop • Café

Works by Futurist artists Balla, Severini and Boccioni are at the heart
of this superb private art collection, amassed by Eric and Salome
Estorick after World War II. Opened in January 1998 and housed in
a beautifully refurbished Georgian building, the museum is easy to
miss when walking by, blending in as it does with the surrounding
architecture. But it is this very domesticity that makes the collection
so exceptional, where the works sit lovingly as part of the furniture.
Going in the evening is particularly atmospheric as the golden
light pours through the window, illuminating the many paintings
and illustrations with an added mystery. If you're not yet sold, the
collection has the distinction of being Britain's first museum devoted
to modern Italian art.

The Estoricks started collecting upon reading Umberto
Boccioni's book *Futurist Painting and Sculpture*, beginning their life-
long love affair with both Italy, and modern Italian art. Eric Estorick
is quoted at the time of visiting the studio of Mario Sironi and
putting 'hundreds of drawings and as many pictures as I could into
my Packard Convertible Roadster'.

While Futurist art forms the core of the collection, other
major 20th-century Italian artists are also represented, including
metaphysical painter Giorgio de Chirico, Giorgio Morandi and master
of the elongated portrait, Amedeo Modigliani. Bronzes by Marino
Marini and Giacomo Manzù are among the featured sculptures.
It's worth noting that displays of the permanent collection change
periodically for conservation reasons.

If you simply don't want to leave (and we don't blame you) there
is a wonderful café space in a glass conservatory, which overlooks
the tranquil gardens. This is an unmissable institution that remains
the quiet king of Islington's art scene.

Fenton House
One of London's great houses
Hampstead Grove, NW3 6SP • 020 7435 3471 • www.
nationaltrust.org.uk/fenton-house-and-garden • Hampstead LU •
Check website for opening hours • £ • Shop

Known primarily for its collection of early keyboard instruments, this National Trust property also contains an interesting array of furniture, textiles, art and 18th-century porcelain, all of which offer a glimpse into the luxurious lifestyle of the house's former inhabitants. Decorated by John Fowler in 1973, the bold tangerine coloured Dining Room forms a vivid backdrop to a group of no less delectable paintings by Sir William Nicholson.

A bequest of 55 paintings, drawings and watercolours from the collection of the late actor Peter Barkworth are an additional draw. Those on permanent display in the house include paintings by the Camden Town School and watercolours by the likes of Constable, Cox and Collier.

A late 17th-century merchant's house, Fenton House retains many original features such as a large walled garden that is bursting with colour and life, and is home to a wonderful collection of rare plants and flowers. Classical concerts are put on here throughout the year and if you're lucky you might hear a music student playing on one of the old spinets or harpsichords during your visit.

Freud Museum London
Last home of the father of psychoanalysis
20 Maresfield Gardens, NW3 5SX • 020 7435 2002 • www.freud.org.uk • Finchley Road LU • Wed-Sun 10.30-17.00 • ££ • Shop

A refugee escaping Nazi oppression, Sigmund Freud made this house his final home. Freud's study, an almost exact recreation of the one he vacated at his apartment in Vienna, remains as it was during his lifetime. Festooned with oriental rugs and lined with books, this room in particular is a remarkable remnant of *fin de siècle* Vienna. The centrepiece of the museum, the study is home to *that* couch as well as to the many Egyptian, Greek, Roman and oriental antiquities Freud loved to collect. Preserved by a long period of burial, these objects from the past are worth seeing in their own right – for the founder of psychoanalysis they constituted the perfect analogy to his own archaeology of the unconscious.

On the landing hangs Salvador Dali's haunting portrait of the face that launched a thousand slips and upstairs there's another couch – this one belonged to Freud's psychoanalyst daughter Anna, who lived at the house and whose pioneering work in child psychoanalysis is also celebrated here. A video shows footage from the Freud family home movies and the shop is well stocked with titles covering the A-Z of psychoanalysis, along with unusual and quirky gifts and jewellery inspired by Freudian theories.

The museum's high calibre temporary exhibitions are also well worth seeing, featuring leading names in contemporary art and literature such as Louise Bourgeois, Mark Wallinger, Alice Anderson, Gavin Turk, Sophie Calle and Tracey Emin. The museum runs an active programme of events relating to Freud and his work and also hosts themed tours at the weekend (see website for further details).

The Jewish Museum

London's only museum dedicated to Jewish history

Raymond Burton House, 129-131 Albert Street, NW1 7NB
• 020 7284 7384 • www.jewishmuseum.org.uk • Camden Town
LU • Sun & Thu 10.00-17.00 • £ • Shop • Café

The museum's outstanding collections of Judaica and Jewish social history follow three themes: an introduction to the Jewish faith, the social history of British Jewry, and the Holocaust.

As the History: A British Story gallery shows, there's been a Jewish presence in London since the Norman invasion of 1066. Displays chart the fortunes of Jews in Britain since then, a cycle of tolerance and persecution that witnessed the expulsion of Jews by Edward I, their welcome back by Cromwell and the 'great Migration' of the 1880s, in which 150,000 Jews fled the pogroms of Eastern Europe to seek refuge in Britain. The East End was the original Jewish heartland in London and there are evocative displays of the trades practiced there by these impoverished migrants – baking equipment, tailor's tools and the ghoulish implements of the furrier.

The museum's Holocaust Gallery focuses on the story of Leon Greenman, a London-born survivor of no less than six concentration camps, fervent anti-racist campaigner and much-loved figure at the museum until his death in 2008. Mr Greenman's photographs and personal possessions are included in the display, some of the most poignant of which relate to his wife and young son, who were both killed within minutes of the family's arrival at Auschwitz.

Judaism: A Living Faith explores the festivals, ethics and rituals of Judaism through the museum's collection of religious ceremonial objects. Items such as an intricately wrought pair of silver 18th-century *kiddush* cups, ornate *rimmonim* (Torah scroll finial), and a magnificent 17th-century Venetian synagogue ark embody the principle of *hiddut mitzvah* or 'beautifying the commandment' and showcase Jewish craftsmanship. Hannukah lamps from around the world reflect the breadth of the Jewish diaspora, allowing visitors to compare and contrast local variations. An interactive exhibit even allows visitors to eavesdrop on a Jewish family's Sabbath meal.

Keats House
Home of the great poet

Keats Grove, NW3 2RR • 020 7332 3868 • www.cityoflondon.
gov.uk/things-to-do/attractions • Hampstead Heath LO • Thu-Fri
& Sun 11.00-13.00, 14.00-16.00 • £ • Shop

Romantic poet par excellence, John Keats lived in this dainty Regency villa from 1818-1820. Despite the onset of tuberculosis that eventually killed him, Keats was at the height of his poetic powers during these years and it was in the garden of Wentworth Place that he penned his *Ode to a Nightingale*. It was here too that he met and fell in love with Fanny Brawne, the "beautiful, elegant, graceful, silly, fashionable and strange" girl next door. They became engaged but the relationship was tragically brief – in September 1820 the ailing poet left Hampstead for the warmer climate of Rome where he died the following February aged just 25. Poignant relics of the doomed love affair include the almandine and gold ring Keats gave Fanny, which she wore for the rest of her life.

Restored to its Regency elegance, the house also commemorates other important relationships in Keats' short life, with a rogues' gallery of literary folk such as Leigh Hunt, Charles Lamb and William Hazlitt. In Keats' day the house was divided with Keats' half being something of a bachelor pad, shared with his friend and landlord Charles Brown. The pair enjoyed a high old time here, hosting 'claret feasts' and card parties. When Keats fell ill, Brown's spacious parlour became Keats' sick room, with a sofa bed placed so he could still look out at the garden. Images of Keats around the house include life and death masks and several posthumous portraits by his friend Joseph Severn, who devotedly nursed the poet in his last months in Rome. The portrait bust of Keats by Anne Whitney in the Brawne Rooms is placed at Keats' actual head height and reveals his tiny stature – just a whisker over 5 feet.

Poetry is still very much a part of Keats House today and the house hosts a poetically-inclined events programme, featuring a high-profile poet in-residence and a summer festival.

Kenwood House

Historic house on the Heath

Hampstead Lane, NW3 7JR • 020 8348 1286 •
www.english-heritage.org.uk • Hampstead Heath LU • Daily
10.00-17.00 • Free • Shop • Café

With its serene neo-Classical architecture, world-class picture
collection, landscaped gardens and extensive catering facilities,
Kenwood is a favourite endpoint for many a Sunday afternoon
walk through Hampstead Heath.

The house, beautifully situated in 112 acres of parkland
created by Sir Humphry Repton, was remodelled for the 1st Earl
of Mansfield by Robert Adam between 1764 and 1779 and it was
here that the Earl raised his illegitimate mixed-race great niece
Dido Belle, whose life was celebrated in the 2014 film *Belle* starring
Gugu Mbatha-Raw. The Earl's anti-slavery rulings in lawsuits of
the time raised eyebrows in some quarters but helped pave the
way for the abolition of slavery some years later.

A major refurbishment in 2013 breathed new life into
Kenwood's Adam interiors, the high point of which is the barrel
vaulted Great Library whose gilded paintwork has been replaced
by Adam's original colour scheme, a delicious confection of pale
pink and blue and icing sugar white. The south front rooms
have also been restored, their décor providing an elegant and
sympathetic backdrop to Kenwood's big draw: the Iveagh Bequest
of paintings. Bequeathed to the nation by the 1st Earl of Iveagh
in 1927, this collection includes gems such as Rembrandt's late,
rather melancholy, self-portrait and Vermeer's *Guitar Player*.
There are frolicksome French paintings by Boucher, portraits by
Van Dyck and plentiful works by British artists, with fine pieces
by the stalwarts of 18th-century portraiture: Gainsborough,
Reynolds and Romney. Three stately 20th-century sculptures
can be admired in the grounds: *Two Piece Reclining Figure No.5* by
Henry Moore, *Empyrean* by Barbara Hepworth and *Flamme* by
Eugene Dodeigne.

Lisson Gallery
Pioneering contemporary gallery
27 Bell Street, NW1 5BY and 67 Lisson Street, NW1 5BU • 020
7724 2739 • www.lissongallery.com • Edgware Road LU • Tue-Sat
11.00-18.00 • Free

Unlike many other galleries in this area, this is a homegrown institution that has since become an international player. Founded in 1967, it still remains in its original site, which was renovated from a derelict building into the stylish gallery space you see today.

When it first opened the gallery pioneered the early careers of important Minimal and Conceptual artists such as Art & Language, Daniel Buren, Donald Judd, John Latham, Sol LeWitt and Robert Ryman. It was also the first gallery to show the work of Anish Kapoor.

Since those early days, Lisson Gallery has gone from strength to strength and now represents a stellar stable of artists including Marina Abramović, Ai Weiwei, John Akomfrah, Susan Hillier, Tatsuo Miyajima and Sean Scully.

Lisson Gallery continues its work promoting a younger generation of artists including Cory Arcangel, Van Hanos and Cheyney Thompson. The gallery certainly stands alone given its location off the Edgware Road and is definitely worth seeking out.

The London Canal Museum
The history of London's commercial waterways
12-13 New Wharf Road, N1 9RT • 020 7713 0836 •
www.canalmuseum.org.uk • King's Cross LU • Wed-Sun 10.00-
16.30 • £ • Shop

Overlooking the murky waters of Regent's Canal, the London
Canal Museum celebrates the history of London's 'silent highway'
from its heyday as a bustling trade route to its more recent role
as a tourist trail. Visitors can experience first hand the cramped
conditions endured by canal folk in part of a restored narrowboat,
admire the distinctive 'roses and castles' artwork that decorated
the narrowboats, and find out how canal locks work.

The building was once a Victorian ice house owned by ice-
cream entrepreneur Carlo Gatti and a massive, still only partially
excavated ice pit dominates the far end of the ground floor.
Displays covering London's ice trade and the history of ice cream
explain the pit's cavernous presence in this canalside warehouse,
and upstairs in the former stables, visitors can sit back and enjoy a
video trip along the canal. The museum's 'Bantam IV' tug is usually
moored at the rear of the museum in the Battlebridge Basin, once
a thriving industrial spot but now a haven of inner city tranquility.

The shop is small but well-stocked with relevant, reasonably-
priced souvenirs, including books about boats and canals and a
range of colourful hand-painted canalware.

If you want to combine this educational visit with a hands-
on-deck experience, in the warmer months visitors can take to
the water for real on narrow boat trips organised by the museum
for an additional fee. You can choose between one hour, ninety
minutes and even full day trips that end in either Victoria Park
or Little Venice. One things for certain, you'll leave the museum
with a newfound appreciation of this defining feature of London's
history and its cityscape.

Queer Britain
Britain's first LGBTQ+ museum
2 Granary Square, N1C 4BH • www.queerbritain.org.uk • King's
Cross LU • Wed-Sun 12.00-18.00 • Free • Shop

Just a stone's throw from London's largest and boldest arts college,
Central Saint Martins, you'll find an equally vibrant establishment
– Queer Britain. New on the scene, this is Britain's first museum
dedicated to LGBTQ+ stories, with its opening marking 50 years
since the first London Pride march.

In this compact but densely informative archive, you'll find
fascinating objects that tell a story of resistance and celebration in
defiance. One such artefact is Oscar Wilde's prison cell door (on
loan from the Museum of Justice) which in its shades of pastel yellow
and turquoise seems as if it was designed to hang in a museum. It
was behind this door that he wrote *De Profundis* on his allocated four
pages a day after being imprisoned under homophobic laws for gross
indecency. Here you can also see one of the dresses worn by the
famous drag queen Divine. But the real highlight is the video room
where they have a steady programme of rarely screened films that
explore queer identities.

However, this is no dusty library; it even had an exhibition launch
party at the iconic institution The Glory. Similarly its promotional
video features as diverse a range of characters as drag queen Bimini
Bon Boulash and TikTok star GK Barry. This is a welcome addition to
London's museum scene and one well worth exploring.

Royal Air Force Museum

A plane-spotter's paradise

Grahame Park Way, NW9 5LL • 020 8205 2266 • www.
rafmuseum.org.uk • Colindale LU • Daily 10.00-17.00 • Free • Café

Set on 10 acres of what was once Hendon aerodrome, this is Britain's national museum dedicated to the RAF. With over 80 historic aircraft, it's a plane-spotter's paradise, as well as a must for those interested in 20th-century history, and particularly the two world wars.

The museum consists of six, sleek barrel vaulted, steel-clad hangers that tell the story of the RAF from its origins in the earliest balloon flight to the latest Eurofighter jet. Other landmark flying machines include flimsy looking early pioneers like the Clarke Glider of 1910 and extend to the legendary Harrier Jump Jet. The list of iconic planes highlights the attractions of seeing these vast technological flying machines up close and personal. In the course of a visit you can 'walk through' a Sunderland flying boat and try your hand at flying a Jet Provost in their simulator. For those less confident about taking the controls there's a 4-D theatre, art gallery and outdoor activity area.

Top Trumps fans will relish the technical specifications that can be accessed via touchscreen computers, along with the history of each aircraft, its designers and pilots and film footage. On the ground floor level visitors can mingle with the machinery, and a quiet moment of contemplation can be sought in the prefab RAF chapel from the Falkland Islands or in front of medals won by airmen.

Prize for the spookiest exhibit goes to the ghostly, water-stained wreck of a Halifax bomber, dredged up from the Norwegian fjord where it had lain since the 1940s. The Hall also serves as a moving memorial to the 131,000 young men who lost their lives during the Allied bombing offensive of World War II.

The Echo Alpha Tango Restaurant and Wessex Café are on standby to banish the inevitable hunger pangs. For those bringing packed lunches, there are picnic areas inside and out. The museum shop has more Airfix models than you can shake a joystick at.

Royal College of Physicians
Medical museum in a Lasdun masterpiece

11 St Andrew's Place, NW1 4LE • 020 3075 1543 • www.history. rcplondon.ac.uk • Great Portland Street LU • Mon-Fri 09.00-17.00 • For groups of 6+ advance booking is necessary • Free

Founded by Henry VIII in 1518, the College is housed in a Grade I listed icon of modern architecture by Sir Denys Lasdun. As the oldest medical college in England it's had plenty of time to build up its heavyweight museum collection which includes the first book printed in the English language. The museum meanwhile gives wall space to some fine portraits of notable physicians past and present – from Zoffany's portrait of William Hunter lecturing, to a sculpture of Sir Raymond Hoffenberg by Dame Elisabeth Frink.

The Hoffbrand collection of English delftware apothecary jars is another must-see here – these attractive earthenware containers shed a fascinating light onto the weird and wonderful substances once regarded as medicine – oil of swallows, anyone? There is also the fascinating Symons collection of medical objects, from nipple shields and tongue scrapers to a stethoscope that belonged to the inventor Rene Laennec. On the upper gallery are a set of anatomical tables – among the oldest surviving human anatomy preparations in Europe.

The museum runs a public programme of talks, lectures, workshops and open days as well hosting two temporary exhibitions a year. The garden is something of a 'living museum' too, and is attractively planted with over 1,300 medicinal plants from around the world.

The Showroom
Commercial gallery commissioning original work
63 Penfold Street, NW8 8PQ • 020 7724 4300 •
www.theshowroom.org • Edgware Road LU • Wed-Sat 12.00-
18.00 • Free

This publicly funded contemporary art gallery, housed in a former
munitions factory, stages several exhibitions a year. The emphasis
is on cross-disciplinary and collaborative shows. Artists, both
homegrown and from abroad, are commissioned to make new work
for the space. Platformed artists earn well-deserved recognition,
like Ciara Phillips' Showroom project which was nominated for the
Turner Prize in 2014.

In 2023 The Showroom hosted an exhibition by artist Oliver
Ressler titled 'Barricading the Ice Sheets'. Ressler's work investigates
the climate crisis through the use of films, photographic works and
live discussions. The show also engaged activists and locals in the
live events and activities which is typical of the gallery's work, with
around 50 public events every year, most of them free to access.

Stephens House & Gardens
Museum dedicated to the Stephens' Ink Company

Avenue House, 17 East End Road, N3 3QE • 020 8346 7812
• www.stephenshouseandgardens.com • Finchley Central LU
• Garden open daily, museum by appointment • Free

Medical man Dr Henry Stephens was the inventor of the famous 'Blue-Black Writing Fluid' and went on to become something big in ink. His son Henry Charles ('Inky') Stephens developed the family business and bought Avenue House in 1874, adding a laboratory and planting the rare trees that can be seen in the landscaped grounds today. Stephens Jr. left the house and gardens to the people of Finchley and it is now run as a charitable trust, with the Stephens Collection being housed in the Old Coach House.

Displays explore the history of the Stephens' Ink Company, and its expansion from Henry's ink boiling experiments in his basement laboratory into a worldwide brand. Its famous 'ink blot' logo was first registered in 1832 and can here been seen on vintage enamel advertising signs, a variety of ink bottles, and innumerable stationery products. Other exhibits recall the fast-disappearing era of fountain pens, blotting paper, ink wells and ink monitors, and delve back further in time to even earlier writing technologies such as papyrus, slate and quills.

A redevelopment project is underway to transform the grounds and improve visitor facilities – something that Finchley resident (and former President of the Finchley Society) Spike Milligan, would no doubt have approved. A life-sized statue of the late Goon sitting on a bench was unveiled in the gardens of Stephens House in 2014 and has become a popular destination for those wanting to 'have a conversation with Spike'.

Victoria Miro
Chic commercial gallery

16 Wharf Road, N1 7RW • 020 7336 8109 • www.victoria-miro.com • Angel LU • Tue-Sat 10.00-18.00 • Free

Victoria Miro has something effortlessly chic about it – the kind of coolness that requires no introduction. But this understated style is matched with the boldness of the art on display. It has gained its reputation humbly and through its consistency of curating unforgettable exhibitions. Housed in an 8,000 square-foot former Victorian furniture factory, it represents established artists such as Turner Prize winners Chris Ofili and Grayson Perry, as well as trail-blazers like Milton Avery and Howardena Pindell.

What sets Victoria Miro apart is its commitment to showcasing artwork that is both visually stunning and thought-provoking. The gallery is not just a space for showcasing art but also a platform for critical conversations about the role of art in society. The staff are knowledgeable and passionate about the art on display and are always on hand to offer insights into the artists' works and answer any questions visitors may have.

The landscaped garden is unmissable. Watching the swans while walking among striking outdoor sculpture (Yayoi Kusama's *Narcissus Garden* is a notable past installation) is a slice of paradise in an otherwise industrial corner of Islington.

Wellcome Collection
Medical museum
183 Euston Road, NW1 2BE • 020 7611 2222 • www.
wellcomecollection.org • Euston Square LU • Check website for
opening hours • Free • Shop • Café & Restaurant

The entrance to the Wellcome is a light and welcoming foyer, complete with an open plan gift shop. It's so welcoming that some visitors may not get beyond this point and for those that decide to pair their visit with a caffeine boost, the expansive café is fit with a forest of dimming and brightening light bulbs priming you for the many 'aha' moments to be had in its exhibition spaces.

The Medicine Man gallery introduces the visitor to Henry Wellcome – an extraordinary character whose entrepreneurial flair took him from humble American log cabin origins to millionaire pharmaceutical business giant and philanthropist. Along the way Wellcome also found time to run major archaeological digs, pioneer aerial photography and amass a 1 million strong collection of medical and cultural artefacts, 500 of which are displayed here. The offbeat cross-section of material takes in everything from serried ranks of amputation saws to 18th-century nipple shields, from Napoleon's toothbrush to a Peruvian mummy. Although the apparently random material is tamed into a dozen or so categories such as 'Masks', there's still a cabinet of curiosity feel about the gallery.

The real star of the show is the Being Human gallery. Designed by Turner Prize-winning collective Assemble, it showcases all that is current in our understandings of health, covering intersectional research and artwork exploring genetics, minds and bodies, infection and most significantly, environmental breakdown. This exhibition space is one of the most interactive and eye-catching in all of London.

Vanitas
Vanitatum et

Zabludowicz Collection

Contemporary gallery in a converted Methodist chapel
176 Prince of Wales Road, NW5 3PT • 020 7428 8940 • www.
zabludowiczcollection.com • Chalk Farm LU • Thu-Sun 12.00-
18.00 • Free • Shop • Café

When you arrive at the collection you will struck by the
gorgeous calm of the surroundings. It's as if Anita Zabludowicz
has engineered the space to be an antidote to frantic gallery
experiences that are all too common. Its minimalist curatorial
approach, and the unique architecture of a converted Methodist
church make this a magnet for contemporary art lovers.

The curved interior and balcony are all original features from
its origins as a church but they make a great exhibition space. Here
you'll find the most cutting-edge and bold of contemporary art,
often with an immersive or VR element to it. Their most recent
exhibition displayed Chinese artist LuYang's work and they even
had the ingenious idea to convert the back room into an arcade
with games the artist had created. This is a gallery that never takes
its reputation for granted, and each exhibition feels pioneering
and fresh.

After entering an altered state, the perfect way to round off
the trip is at their great value café. With great coffee there is no
excuse not to enjoy their outside seating overlooking this leafy
Camden neighbourhood.

2 Willow Road
Goldfinger's remarkable modernist house

Willow Road, Hampstead, NW3 1TH • 020 7435 6166 • www.nationaltrust.co.uk• Belsize Park LU • Thu & Sat 11.00-14.00 • £

A Modernist interpretation of a terraced house, 2 Willow Road is as about as far from the stereotype of a National Trust property as it's possible to get. Set in leafy Hampstead, it was built by architect Ernö Goldfinger in 1937 and remained his family home until 1994. It is one of only two Modernist houses in the country that are open to the public. The stylish Modernist aesthetic of the building is matched by its contents – along with furniture and toys designed by Goldfinger are works of art by Henry Moore, Bridget Riley, Max Ernst and Marcel Duchamp.

Goldfinger's uncompromising approach is not everyone's cup of tea – his Trellick Tower in North Kensington remains controversial although flats inside are still much sought after. An introductory video is shown at regular intervals.

Don't forget to check out the rooftop terrace, which offers stunning views of Hampstead and the surrounding areas. It's the perfect spot to sit and relax, taking in the splendour of the surrounding landscape while admiring the architectural beauty of the house.

The house is a true masterpiece, a testament to Goldfinger's vision and talent, and a rare opportunity to see an architectural gem preserved in its original state. It is necessary to pre-book: the first half of the day is by guided tour only and from 3pm onwards you can explore the property independently.

Leighton House

West

The Alexander Fleming Laboratory Museum
Tiny museum dedicated to a big discovery
St Mary's Hospital, Praed Street, W2 1NY • www.medicalmuseums.
org/Alexander-Fleming-Laboratory Museum • Paddington LU •
Mon-Thu 10.00-13.00 • Free • Shop

It was in this tiny, old-fashioned laboratory that Alexander Fleming discovered penicillin – a storm in a petri dish - that transformed its discoverer into a national hero and earned him a Nobel Prize.

A very distant relation to today's pristine white boxes, the laboratory is an accurate reconstruction of Fleming's workplace (although his original penicillin culture plate is housed at the British Library). If microbiology isn't your forte you needn't worry as the museum kick starts with a comprehensive clip that charts the entire history of penicillin, often described as the "single greatest victory ever achieved over disease".

The exhibition then charts the development of penicillin from mystery mould to life-saving wonder drug and the impact of antibiotics on modern medicine. But as the saying (kind of) goes, a spoonful of humour makes the medicine go down, and the display also explores the sillier sides of research before the age of red tape and supervision. There is one account of a lab assistant tasting the 'mould juice' from the penicillin to see if it was toxic, remarking that it tasted just like stilton. If you want a more in-depth understanding of all things Fleming then they also offer explanatory tours tailored to visitors needs. Here visitors are guided through the momentous – and accidental – discovery of penicillin.

In recounting the details of Fleming's life and career the museum reveals oddities such as reproductions of the bizarre 'germ' paintings he created and mould medallions given names like Queen Elizabeth, Winston Churchill and Marlene Dietrich. With artefacts like Fleming's first microscope, this museum is a remarkable exploration of one of the world's most important medical discoveries.

Chiswick House & Gardens
A neo-Palladian masterpiece
Burlington Lane, W4 2RP • 020 8995 0508 • www.chgt.org.uk•
Chiswick Rail • Thu-Sun 11.00-16.00 (Garden open daily) • £
• Café

The last word in classical chic when it was built in the 1720s, Chiswick House is still a sumptuously stylish pad by any standards. Owner-architect Lord Burlington was inspired by the architecture of ancient Rome and Renaissance architect Andrea Palladio. An enthusiastic 'grand tourist', Burlington returned home from his travels with 878 trunks of art acquisitions and set about designing a building that would represent the different aspects of Roman architecture: domestic, religious and civic. The result is his masterpiece – a villa that was intended not as a home, but rather as an art gallery and severely upmarket party pad.

The interiors centre around the octagonal domed 'tribunal' and include the resplendent Red, Green and Blue Velvet Rooms – the latter being Burlington's study, whose royal blue and gold colour scheme makes Lady Burlington's perfectly pleasant bed chamber look rather dowdy in comparison. A pair of original 'Chiswick' tables designed by Burlington's artistic collaborator William Kent are among the treasures on display, along with a set of paintings of Chiswick House in the 18th century by Rysbrack. The historic gardens, also designed by William Kent, are often described as the birthplace of the English landscape movement, and are just as much of a draw as the house.

A much-loved resource for the local community, the gardens are free to the public and open every day. They are a popular haunt for dog walkers, who even organise an annual dog show, complete with celebrity judges. Refreshments for human visitors can be tracked down at the sleek contemporary café, designed by award-winning architects Caruso St John. The thriving 17th-century kitchen garden grows an abundance of fruit, veg and flowers, which are sold from the Conservatory Shop.

The Design Museum
A shrine to design
Kensington High Street, W8 6NQ • www.designmuseum.org
• High Street Kensington LU • £ • Shops • Café & Restaurant

A shrine to contemporary design and architecture, the Design Museum with its swooping paraboloid copper roof is a west London landmark. Since first opening in Shad Thames in 1989 it has championed the role of good design and showcased the work of designers such as Charles and Ray Eames, Zaha Hadid and Sir Paul Smith; its displays of iconic designs have embraced everything from an AK-47 to Lady Gaga's bin-bag dress.

In 2016 the museum relocated to the former Commonwealth Institute that underwent a multi-million redevelopment by architect John Pawson. Its new home is a masterpiece of concrete, wood and steel and has allowed the museum to spread its wings and fly. In recent years the museum has hosted some of London's most memorable exhibitions, notably the 2019 retrospective of the life and work of film director Stanley Kubrick.

More recently it hosted *WEIRD SENSATION FEELS GOOD: The World of ASMR*. The exhibition featured a room devoted to Bob Ross and his cult classic *The Joy of Painting*, that could be watched via five TV's, and was one of 2022's standout cultural experiences.

Just looking through their colourful archive of exhibitions you get a taste of the sheer scope of what's on offer: from Ai Wei Wei's relationship to design in *Making Sense* to the *off beat sari* – an exploration of the modern role of the sari. There are also blockbuster affairs like Alexander McQueen's *30 Years of London Fashion* – as much a love letter to the city as to the man himself.

The permanent exhibition *Design Maker User* snakes around the open plan space and tells the story of thousands of the most influential designs of the modern world, from the Industrial Revolution to the present day. The 'Design' section has a particular focus on the designers who formed both the aesthetic and practical building-blocks of London life like David Mellor's traffic light, the British road signage system devised by Kinneir and Calvert, and a life-sized model of the new London tube train designed by PriestmanGoode. 'Makers' tells the story of industrialization and manufacturing through its display of works at different stages of production from the Model T Ford to robotic arms, mass customisation and 3D printing. In the last section 'User' things become a little more familiar, and there's plenty for misty-eyed nostalgics to enjoy here, including the first iMac bubble computer and the Sony Walkman, to gorgeous classics like the Olivetti Valentine typewriter and a Dieter Rams vinyl player. No stone is left unturned and it does a great job at giving a sweeping overview of the history of design.

If all these beautiful objects make you want to shop till you drop, you needn't worry for they have three on-site shops: on the high street, in the atrium, and in the gallery. The gift shops stay true to the ethos of 'good design' with more minimalist displays. In the gallery shop you'll find a balance of books, gizmos and unusually some of the current on-trend objects of design, like a 'WasteBoard Skateboard' made of recycled plastic caps.

If you need some rest and relaxation after all this design inspiration the museum has dining options that cater for every occasion, from relaxed snacks and drinks to the Parabola restaurant that offers a seasonal, locally-sourced menu with wonderful views over west London.

The Design Museum has certainly been enhanced by the move to West London and remains one of the most iconic London institutions that should really not be missed.

Hogarth's House
Home of the great British artist

Hogarth Lane, Great West Road, Chiswick, W4 2QN
• 020 8994 6757 • www.hounslow.info/arts/hogarthshouse
• Turnham Green LU • Tue-Sun 12.00-17.00 • Free • Shop

From the outside, it takes a leap of imagination to picture this quaint red brick house back in the 18th century when it was the home of the painter-engraver William Hogarth. Only one room deep, the house was described by Hogarth as his 'little country box by the Thames', a place where he and his family could enjoy a more relaxed pace of life away from his town house and studio in Leicester Fields. Today Hogarth's rural retreat looks out over the less than tranquil pastures of the A4 and the roundabout that bears his name, but the charming walled garden remains and contains a craggy old mulberry tree that Hogarth would have known.

Often regarded as the father of British painting, Hogarth's fame now rests on the detailed social observation and scathing moral commentaries of engravings such as *The Rake's Progress*, *Marriage à la Mode* and *Gin Lane*, some of which are displayed throughout the house.

Hogarth's interests were wide-ranging and as well as setting up an art academy and being responsible for the first copyright legislation, he was a philanthropist, instrumental in setting up the Foundling Hospital. The Hogarths fostered several children and in the summer had foundling children to stay with them at Chiswick, where Mrs Hogarth would apparently bake them mulberry pies using berries from the tree in the garden.

Hogarth's House has undergone several refurbishments over the years. The most recent has been a Heritage Lottery funded extension to the museum, incorporating a new multi-purpose learning studio and garden refurbishment adding a skittle alley, garden trail and an imaginative replanting of the existing garden. The improvements add to the appeal of a museum that is definitely worth seeking out.

Kensington Palace

Royal residence designed by Wren

Kensington Gardens, W8 4PX • 0844 482 7777 • www.hrp.org.
uk/KensingtonPalace• High Street Kensington LU • Wed-Sun
10.00-18.00 • £££ • Shop • Café and Restaurant

Kensington Palace was bought by King William III and Queen Mary II in 1689 when it was still humble Nottingham House. Remodelled for them by Sir Christopher Wren, this tidy red brick building has been a much-loved home to a succession of royals ever since: Queen Victoria and Diana, Princess of Wales among them. The palace underwent a multi-million pound refurbishment to reopen in time for the Queen's Diamond Jubilee in 2012 and the public half of Kensington Palace can now be explored via four different routes, which tell the stories of some of the monarchs who have lived here.

The new displays have been curated with a light touch and friendly real-life 'explainers' are on hand to give talks throughout the day but will happily answer questions in between.

For a chronological tour, start with the Queen's State Apartments, built for Queen Mary II in the 17th century. These homely wood-panelled rooms were once filled with Mary's menagerie of pet dogs and birds. Altogether grander, the King's State Apartments were created by the Hanoverian monarchs and feature lavish interiors by William Kent. The King's Gallery doubled up as an indoor exercise yard and a picture gallery while the King's Drawing Room was the scene of courtly socialising and high-risk card games. Cultured Queen Caroline preferred the Privy Chamber for entertaining: it features a superb ceiling decoration by William Kent depicting the Roman gods Mars and Minerva. An illusionistic tour de force, *The King's Staircase*, was also painted by Kent, and is peopled by real-life court characters, such as Wild Peter, a feral child who lived at the Palace, and the artist himself.

The Kensington Palace features a pleasant self-service café, while the revamped shop is stocked with tasteful souvenirs. A short stroll away, the Orangery Restaurant offers a more elegant dining experience, and is a popular destination for afternoon tea.

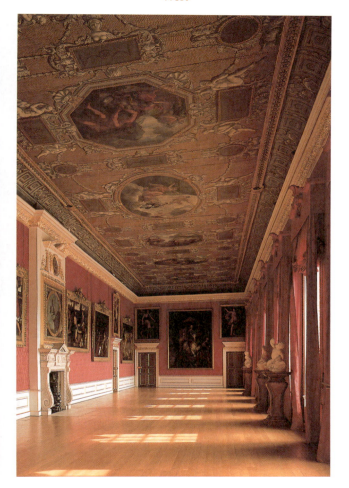

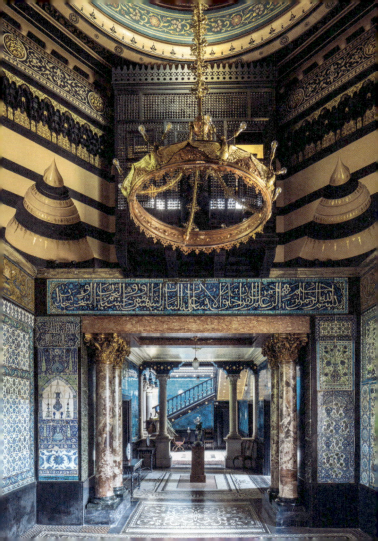

Leighton House
Idiosyncratic home of Lord Leighton
12 Holland Park Road, W14 8LZ • 020 7602 3316 • www.rbkc.
gov.uk/museums • Kensington Olympia LO • Wed-Mon 10.00-
17.30 • ££ • Café

Fresh from its recent £8 million refurbishment, this evocative haute-
bohemian pad was once home to Frederic, Lord Leighton, the great
classical painter of the Victorian age. Hung with paintings by the
man himself and his Pre-Raphaelite pals Millais and Burne-Jones,
and with ceramics by William de Morgan, the house was designed
as a palace devoted to art, and its opulent interiors are spellbinding.

Leighton's vast studio dominates the upper floor with its high
ceiling and large north-facing windows that flood the space with
natural light. It's easy to imagine Leighton at work here, surrounded
by his paints and canvases. This room allows you to enter the mind
of the artist with its preserved paints and canvases, frozen in time.
You then travel from the creative process to the finished work, with
numerous examples of his art decorating the walls.

The domed Arab Hall is the centrepiece of the house: a Moorish
fantasia complete with gilt mosaic frieze, antique Iznik tiles, lattice-
work mashrabiyah' window and gently playing fountain. An award-
winning refurbishment and restoration has returned Lord Leighton's
interiors to their polychrome 19th-century glory, with specially
commissioned wall coverings for the silk room and the dining room.

A hugely successful artist in his day, Leighton entertained the
great and good of the Victorian art world in his flamboyant home but
it is instructive to compare and contrast the splendour of the 'public'
rooms with the austere simplicity of Leighton's sparsely furnished
bedroom. Don't forget to visit the new addition, De Morgan Café,
which looks over the gorgeous gardens.

The Museum of Brands

A shopping trip down memory lane

111-117 Lancaster Road, W11 1QT • 020 7243 9611 • www.
museumofbrands.com • Ladbroke Grove LU • Mon-Sat 10.00-
18.00, Sun 11.00-17.00 • £ • Shop • Café

This delightfully eccentric museum is the brainchild of Robert Opie
and pays affectionate homage to 20th century consumerism or, as
the Wombles would have it, the 'everyday things that folks leave
behind'. Robert Opie's eureka moment occurred at the age of 16 and
involved, of all things, a Munchies' wrapper. From this humble start
his collection has grown to comprise thousands of items, including
toys, packaging, and advertising artwork. The permanent collection
is laid out as a timeline that snakes its way from the 1890s to the
present day and provokes delighted cries of recognition as visitors
re-encounter the toys, sweets and games of their childhood. A TV
room, playing old television adverts, offers another portal into our
– and advertising's – past.

Nostalgia aside, the collection deftly shows how consumerism
reflects society, unerringly charting trends like our national
obsession with crisps, ready meals and washing whiter than white.
Striking a chord with current concerns about over-packaging,
displays examine the technology and materials of packaging itself,
from earthenware to Tetrapak, and explore the evolution of well-
known brands. Commercial artwork is a particular strength of
the collection and the flowing Art Nouveau lines of an Edwardian
biscuit tin, or the striking Art Deco cover of a 1920s Radio Times
show how directly the art movements of the day affected the look
of ephemeral everyday items. The displays of vintage fashions
through the decades – from flapper dress to mini skirt – have
been expanded and reflect Opie's view of clothing as the ultimate
human packaging. The shop stocks an appealing range of nostalgic
products and the tearoom has a garden, with lush plants and
outdoor seating.

Diamond Jubilee 1897

Sixty glorious years were celebrate

FORMATION

The National Army Museum
Museum dedicated to the British and Commonwealth soldier
Royal Hospital Road, SW3 4HT • 020 7730 0717 • www.nam.ac.uk • Sloane Square LU • Free • Shop • Café

If you've got a thing about men – or women – in uniform, this is the place for you. Unlike the Imperial War Museum whose subject is 20th and 21st century conflict, the NAM focuses on the life of ordinary British and Commonwealth soldiers and is appropriately situated next to the Royal Hospital, home of the Chelsea Pensioners. It also has the acclaim of holding the largest collection of artefacts relating to the British Army, preserving over 350 years of history right up to the present day.

If you've ever had a morbid curiosity about what life was like for a soldier on the front line (let's face it, we all have), the museum recreates the sounds and smells of battle with its immersive exhibits, providing visitors with a visceral understanding of the challenges and dangers faced by soldiers throughout history.

Fear not, this isn't just *Call of Duty* with an educational twist and the museum's narrative is balanced in its exploration of war and conflict throughout time, allowing visitors to make up their own mind about the achievements of the military. For example, the recent exhibition 'Foe to Friend' followed the lives of German soldiers and how Anglo-Germanic relations have developed. It's exhibitions and Conflict in Europe gallery seek to humanize the history of war and explain international relations in a non-partisan way.

The museum makes for a fantastic family day out, educational and fun in equal measure with events like 'Soldier Stories': dramatically re-enacted life stories from the Army's past as well as their play base for children 8 and under. There is also plenty for hungry adult minds to feast on with their fascinating programme of talks and workshops like a recent talk hosted by Dr. Diya Gupta exploring the history of India in World War II.

The National Army Museum is a much-needed institution and an incredible opportunity to find out more about Britain's role in warfare in the past, present and future.

The Natural History Museum
Museum dedicated to nature
Cromwell Road, SW7 5BD • 020 7942 5000 • www.nhm.ac.uk •
South Kensington LU • Daily 10.00-17.50 • Free • Shops
• Restaurant & Café

One of South Kensington's 'Big Three' museums, the Natural History Museum has been a London landmark since 1881. Famed for its dinosaur and fossil collections, the museum has evolved into one of London's most popular attractions, welcoming over 5 million visitors a year as well as supporting a 300-strong team of research scientists behind the scenes.

Purpose built by Alfred Waterhouse, the original museum building on Cromwell Road is worth a visit in its own right. Its elegant Romanesque arches conceal an iron and steel framework – the last word in Victorian structural innovation – but it is Waterhouse's lavish use of terracotta that really distinguishes the building. Beautifully detailed sculptures of plants and animals liberally adorn both the interior and exterior of the museum, carefully distinguishing between living and extinct species (which were originally segregated in west and east wings respectively).

For decades Hintze Hall has been dominated by an iconic Diplodocus skeleton cast but 'Dippy' is now on long-term loan and has been permanently replaced by a 25-metre-long blue whale skeleton called *Hope* that is equally awe-inspiring. Dippy may have lost the top spot but the always busy Dinosaurs gallery is chock-a-block with equally oversized skeletons. The gallery is popular with young visitors, keen to walk amongst 'fearful lizards' like Dromaeosaurus, Triceratops and the mighty Tyrannosaurus Rex.

Interactive displays look at possible reasons for their eventual demise. The Dino Store is handily placed opposite the exit, for those looking for a themed souvenir to take home. There's more animal magic, albeit of the stuffed variety, in 'Mammals'. Outlandish flying mammals and mammals with pouches put in an appearance alongside more familiar species, such as dogs. Films and hands-on exhibits supplement the taxidermy and bring to life the various

mammalian habits, life cycles and evolution. 'Images of Nature' shows highlights from the museum's collection of over half a million natural history artworks – from delicately nuanced drawings to ultra-close-up images captured via electron microscopes.

The massive cross section of a 1,300-year-old giant sequoia at the top of the Hintze Hall puts our puny human lifespans into perspective. Date markers chart major events like the Battle of Hastings and the foundation of Islam against its numerous growth rings. The Treasure Gallery that opened at the end of 2012, offers a snapshot of the museum in one jewel-like room. Among the precious exhibits are an Emperor Penguin egg collected on Scott's fateful last Antarctic expedition, two birds that are as dead as dead can be (the extinct dodo and great auk), a piece of the moon, and plant specimens collected on Captain Cook's first voyage to Australia.

Over on the western flank of the museum, the Darwin Centre is a state-of-the-art research station that houses somewhere in the region of 22 million specimens, and rather fewer live scientists. Here visitors can embark on a Cocoon tour, following a gently sloping walkway around the outside of the vast storage 'cocoon', past beautifully displayed insect and plant specimens as well as a sequence of high-tech interactive displays. Visitors are introduced to the influential natural history collector, Sir Hans Sloane, and invited to explore the fundamentals of the science of nature. Aimed at adults and older students, slick touchscreen interactives allow you to play at being a scientist, leaf through a herbarium and plan a field trip. The real versions can be seen hard at work in the adjacent laboratories and down on the ground floor in the Angela Marmont Centre for UK Nature, while the David Attenborough Studio hosts films and lectures.

The Natural History Museum is always evolving and at present the Wildlife Gardens are undergoing a major transformation, which will double the area of natural habitats. Visitors can seek solace from the garden's temporary closure at the Darwin Centre café, one of several cafés and the perfect place to round off your visit.

Pitzhanger Manor & Gallery
Grand weekend retreat of Sir John Soane
Mattock Lane, W5 5EQ • 020 8567 1227 • www.pitzhanger.org.
uk • Ealing Broadway LU • Free • Café

Pitzhanger Manor was built by architect Sir John Soane as his weekend retreat in the early 1800s. A rare example of a Regency villa in Ealing, the manor exemplifies Soane's elegant and stripped back style of Neo-classical architecture – other examples in London include Dulwich Picture Gallery (see p.216) and Sir John Soane's Museum (see p.98). The interiors of the manor house are a treat for the senses, with intricate plasterwork, richly carved woodwork, and luxurious furnishings. The spaces are designed to immerse visitors in the opulence and grandeur of the Georgian era, while also providing a fascinating insight into Soane's own tastes and aesthetic philosophy.

The Soane Gallery, recently restored to great acclaim, is a testament to Soane's innovative and visionary approach to design. The gallery space is host to contemporary artists who interract with the Georgian space and produce a stunning contrast of modern and traditional. Most recently Anthony Caro's *The Inspiration of Architecture* provided an interesting dialogue and dynamism to the space. Pitzhanger is so much more than a historical preservation and has a lively programme of life drawing classes, sculpture workshops, family-friendly Sundays and even yoga classes.

A visit here can easily become a full-day affair with the charming on-site café: the Pitzhanger Pantry offering a variety of hot and cold drinks, sandwiches, salads, and pastries. With plenty of outdoor seating, it's the perfect spot to relax and overlook luscious Walpole park.

Pitzhanger Manor & Gallery is now easily accessible on the Elizabeth line and offers a one-of-a-kind immersive experience and an unmissable window into the world of one of England's most celebrated architects and his enduring legacy.

The Saatchi Gallery
Cutting edge art just off King's Road
Duke of York's HQ, King's Road, SW3 4RY • 020 7811 3070 •
www.saatchigallery.com • Sloane Square LU • Daily 10.00-18.00
• Free / £££ for visiting exhibitions • Shop

Since 1985, Saatchi has showcased the work of emerging artists and acquired a strong reputation for introducing artists who would later gain worldwide recognition. The gallery has been housed in this elegantly renovated ex-army premises since October 2008 and in 2019 became a registered charity.

With 70,000 square feet of white-walled and wooden-floored gallery space there's plenty of room to show off this renowned and ever-developing contemporary art collection in a series of snappily titled temporary exhibitions. Controversial Brit-Art may be what the Saatchi is best known for in the popular imagination but the collection is truly international in scope and recent shows include 'The New Black Vanguard, America in Crisis' and 'Vision and Virtuosity by Tiffany and Co'.

From the archive 'Sweet Harmony' in 2019 surveyed rave culture through those that lived it, with a particular focus on acid house. It included a disco room where people could get their boogie on, netted entrances that mimicked raves and a Lotus Esprit rotating from the ceiling. This unforgettable exhibition was of the calibre expected of the Saatchi.

For all the conspicuous consumption on display along the King's Road, the gallery has a surprisingly egalitarian approach and is committed to supporting new artists and making contemporary art accessible to all. The visiting exhibitions are reasonably priced and there is a busy programme of talks and workshops.

For those who prefer to enjoy culture with a drink in hand, check out monthly Saatchi Lates, which include talks and workshops. Coinciding with their new charitable status, the Saatchi opened the Learning Gallery, which engages diverse audiences through participatory projects.

The Science Museum
Institution dedicated to invention
Exhibition Road, SW7 2DD • 0870 870 4868 • www.
sciencemuseum.org.uk • South Kensington LU • Daily 10.00-18.00
• Free / £ for temporary exhibitions • Shop • Cafés

You don't have to be a brainbox to enjoy a visit to the Science Museum – indeed its reputation has been built by its accessible curation and information. Its engaging and dynamic displays take a broad view of historic and contemporary science, encompassing technology, industry, medicine and more.

With over 425,000 objects within the collection, the museum prides itself on its interactive exhibits, many of which are geared towards children. Down in the basement 'The Garden' is a discovery area for 3–6 year olds. Also here 'The Secret Life of the Home' is an entertaining display charting man's struggle to conquer the domestic front. Given the technological wizardry on show elsewhere in the museum, the evolution of the humble toilet is a funny contrast – culminating in a frank presentation of how a modern flush loo works.

On the ground floor 'Exploring Space' is a popular attraction covering early rocketeers, men on the moon and modern satellite communications. The Black Arrow satellite launcher looms large and there's also a look at life in space – only 50 miles away – complete with astronauts' undies and a Coke can specially adapted for gravity-free conditions.

'Technicians' on the first floor is an new gallery space exploring the importance of those that apply technology to the modern world from lighting set engineers in the film industry to NHS pharmacy technicians creating life saving medicines. There's even a career area for young visitors wanting to find out about working in different technical fields from wind turbines to design.

The new Energy Revolution gallery takes a detailed look at the climate crisis and the energy revolution needed to reduce our dependence on fossil fuels. The gallery draws on the museum's vast collection to explore the history of energy use, the use of climate modelling and how new energies will transform our way of living.

Science and art come together in the Clockmakers' Museum on the 2nd floor. This museum within a museum showcases the collection of the Worshipful Company of Watchmakers, the oldest of its kind in the world. It's a welcome contrast with many of the interactive displays in the museum to see case after case of carefully calibrated timepieces. The gallery is testament to London's history as a centre of watch making excellence. Among the treasures is the watch worn by Sir Edmund Hillary on his Everest ascent.

Contained within a vast hangar-like space, 'Flight' takes off on the 3rd floor. Flying machines of all descriptions hang from the ceiling like Airfix models – from papery biplanes to Britain's first jet plane. A high-level walkway gives a bird's-eye view of the planes, which include several historic exhibits from the pioneering days of flight, such as the *Vickers Vimy* in which Alcock and Brown crossed the Atlantic in 1919.

Contemporary science is the name of the game in the West Hall. Its exhibitions handle the hottest topics in science today such as genetics, digital technology, and artificial intelligence. 'Who am I?' is a bio-medical investigation into identity and brain science with a Live Science area with fun interactive bloids. The under 8's haven't been forgotten either – the importance of patterns in science is the premise for 'Pattern Pod', a multi-sensory exhibit. There's also a ticketed interactive children's gallery – Wonderlab – with live shows and demonstrations designed to inspire young minds. Looming large on the third floor, the IMAX cinema shows science films such as *Hubble 3D* and *Antartica 3D* on its five storey-high screen.

For children who just can't tear themselves away, the museum organises Astronights sleepover events with demonstrations, hands-on workshops and gallery trails.

If all that thinking makes you peckish, there are several on-site cafés as well as picnic sites with seating dotted about the museum to enjoy a snack on the go.

Sambourne House
A perfectly preserved Victorian home
18 Stafford Terrace, W8 7BH • 020 7361 3790 • www.rbkc.gov.
uk/museums • High Street Kensington LU • Wed-Sun 10.00-17.30
• ££ • Shop

A hidden Victorian gem in the heart of London. Remarkably well-preserved and complete with its original interior decoration and contents, Sambourne House is one of London's best kept secrets. From 1875, this time capsule of a terraced house was the home of Punch illustrator and cartoonist Edward Linley Sambourne, his wife Marion, their two children and live-in servants.

Originally decorated by the Sambournes in keeping with fashionable aesthetic principles, the interiors evolved into wonderfully eclectic artistic statement. And yet, the house remains within the confines of a Victorian middle-class home – jam-packed with pictures, ornaments and knick-knacks of all sorts.

Each room tells a story, from the elegant drawing room to the charming bedrooms, and you can easily imagine the lives of the Victorian family who once lived here. But the true highlight is Edward Linley's cartoonist's studio, which has been restored to its former glory and offers a fascinating insight into his creative process through the intricate sketches and drawings on display.

The guided tour of the house is led by their knowledgeable and enthusiastic staff providing a wealth of information about the house's history and its former residents. The tour concludes with a visit to the gift shop, where if you're struggling to pry yourself from the space there are plenty of books, souvenirs, and prints inspired by Sambourne's artwork to take the essence of the house home with you.

Serpentine
Art in a royal park

Kensington Gardens, W2 3XA & West Carriage Drive, W2 2AR
• 020 7402 6075 • www.serpentinegalleries.org • Lancaster Gate
LU • Tue-Sun 10.00-18.00 • Free • Shop

Art and nature combine at this publicly funded art gallery. Set in the pastoral 18th-century landscape of Hyde Park, Serpentine provides a relaxed and informal location for viewing exemplary contemporary art. In 2013 Serpentine's original exhibition space (a 1930s tea pavilion) was doubled in size by the opening of Serpentine North (a former 19th-century gunpowder store), five-minutes walk away. The new gallery was designed by the late architect Zaha Hadid as a space for specially commissioned work and a shop and included a billowing fibreglass extension for a new café.

Exhibitions at Serpentine are often challenging and controversial but always worth seeing; recent shows have profiled Michael Craig Martin, Louise Bourgeois, Anish Kapoor, Paula Rego and Wolgang Tillmans. The gallery famously hosted a sleeping Tilda Swinton in Cornelia Parker's work *The Maybe*.

Every summer the gallery commissions a 'pavilion', a temporary structure designed by some of the hottest names in contemporary architecture (Frank Gehry, Jean Nouvel, and Herzog & de Meuron, the architects behind Tate Modern, are just some of those who have contributed to this ongoing venture). Playful, provocative, and good fun, the pavilions are sometimes the architect's first completed work in the UK. A full and varied programme of events accompanies the exhibitions – look out for the 24-hour Serpentine Marathon, a day-long series of presentations on a given theme by artists and scientists from all disciplines.

The Serpentine is an incredible art space and one made all the more attractive by the lush surroundings of Hyde Park. A visit to the remarkable café is strongly recommended. It offers the chance to admire one of Zaha Hadid's few London buildings and will also be the site for an annual mural project, which began with the site specific work of the late Atta Kwami.

Tate Britain

Millbank institution dedicated to British art
Millbank, SW1P 4RG • 020 7887 8888 • www.tate.org.uk
Pimlico LU • Daily 10.00-18.00 • Free / ££££ for visiting
exhibitions • Shops • Café & Restaurant

Housed beside the Thames on the one-time site of Millbank Prison, Tate Britain is the national gallery of British art. The gallery opened in 1897, officially becoming the 'Tate Gallery' in 1932. Evolution seems to have been part of the Tate's DNA from its earliest days; regional outposts of the burgeoning Tate empire sprang up in Liverpool and St Ives in the 1980s and 90s, but the biggest shift came in the new millennium with the arrival of Tate Modern. After its collection of modern international art was installed, the Tate Gallery was rebranded Tate Britain and returned to its original focus on homegrown art.

Recently, Tate Britain has shouldered some controversy regarding the Rex Whistler mural *The Expedition in Pursuit of Rare Meats*, commissioned in 1926 and found in the former Tate restaurant. Its depictions of slavery and racist caricatures caused outcry when brought to public attention. While the restaurant is now closed, Tate have decided to commission a new work in dialogue with the mural while retaining it, with an artist yet to be announced.

Since then Tate has completely shaken things up in the most significant rehang in their history. Through interventions, captions and a more diverse array of artists; empire, sexual identity and gender are interrogated. Now half of all contemporary works are from women artists and many notable ones from before the 20th century have been purchased, including many by Joan Carlisle, the first woman in Britain to work as a professional oil painter.

The permanent collection spans some 500 years from the Renaissance to the present day and features works by the lynchpins of British art including Hogarth and Moore, as well as contemporary names such as Riley and Parker. In contrast to the thematic approach adopted at Tate Modern, Tate Britain has a chronological presentation – an absorbing, century-by-century,

sometimes decade-by-decade snapshot of what the Brits have been painting, drawing and sculpting. Since the 2023 rehanging many of the rooms have undergone interventions by a contemporary work. For example, in the Exiles and Dynasties room (1545-1640), Mona Hartoum's *Exodus 2* (2002) – a pair of suitcases joined by strands of human hair – becomes a commentary on the experience of exile that many of the (mostly unknown) artists displayed here would have experienced as refugees from northern Europe.

Another addition is two new permanent rooms of two unexpected artists in conversation: William Blake and Chris Ofili. Blake's work, which since their 2019 exhibition has achieved greater acclaim, is juxtaposed against a room dedicated to Ofili's contemporary watercolours and sketches that similarly have magical and mythological elements to them like *Harvester*.

But it's still the Tate we know and love, featuring classic images like John Singer Sargent's *Carnation, Lily, Lily Rose*, as well as iconic contemporary pieces like *The Splash* by David Hockney and Tracey Emin's unforgettable *My Bed*. As befitting the period in which Tate Britain was founded, there is a spectacular collection of Pre-Raphaelite paintings, including *Ophelia* by Sir John Everett.

A vibrant programme of temporary exhibitions complements the permanent collection, such as the recent show 'Isaac Julien: What Freedom is to Me'. And proving that new art isn't just the preserve of Tate Modern, every year Britain's highest profile contemporary art contest the Turner Prize is awarded here to a British artist under 50. With all the hype, it's easy to overlook the work of its namesake, JMW Turner, whose bequest to the nation is housed in the purpose-built Clore Gallery, revealing Turner in all his guises, from the artist's only self-portrait, to grand classical compositions such as *Dido and Aeneas*, and sublimely Romantic subjects such as *The Fall of an Avalanche in the Grisons*.

For those planning a double dose of Tate, a fast boat service runs between Tate Britain and Tate Modern capitalising on both venues' riverside locations.

Victoria and Albert Museum
The world's largest museum of applied art and design
Cromwell Road, South Kensington, SW7 2RL • 020 7942 2000 •
www.vam.ac.uk • South Kensington LU • Daily 10.00-17.45 • Free
/ £££ for temporary exhibitions • Shops • Café & Restaurant

In May 1899, Queen Victoria laid the foundation stone that would mark the beginning of this museum and the end of her public ceremonies, as she would die two years later. While this was the birth of the V&A as we know it, the roots of the museum actually began in the Great Exhibition of 1851. One of the minds behind this venture was Henry Cole, who became the director of the V&A and its earlier incarnation as Museum of Manufacturers. It's humble core collection was made up of £5000 worth of objects from the Great Exhibition, carrying its ethos of celebrating the best of industry and manufacturing. It has since expanded to be a 21st century shrine to all manners of art and design, packed with beautiful textiles and fashion, jewellery, ceramics, glass and furniture from across the centuries and around the globe, and has long been cherished by creatives, for whom it acts as an inspirational source book.

With a whopping 150 galleries, newcomers may find comfort in the free guided hour-long tours that depart daily from the information desk. Maps are available but unplanned detours in this labyrinthine museum are all part of the fun – you are bound to find something of interest, including whole galleries you may not have encountered before.

The V&A's collections are grouped into five major themes: Asia, Europe, Materials and Techniques, Modern and Exhibitions. Highlights include the vast 16th century Ardabil Carpet – the largest Islamic carpet in existence, the eerie skeletal façade of Sir Paul Pindar's house – a rare wooden survivor of the Great Fire of London, and an exact recreation of Kylie Minogue's dressing room from her *Showgirl* tour.

The British galleries comprise 15 galleries and 3,000 exhibits, and examine how Britain rose from design non-entity to become

'the workshop of the world'. Covering the years 1500-1900 AD, the displays feature five completely restored period rooms such as the 18th century Norfolk Music Room as well as furniture, metalwork, ceramics, textiles, fine art and old favourites such as the Great Bed of Ware and the Stoke Edith Hangings. These galleries include discovery areas with hands-on exhibits and a study space.

Seven new Europe 1600-1815 galleries opened in December 2015 and explore themes such as The Enlightenment, Balloonmania and local traditions. Five years in the making, these are well worth making a beeline for.

Sculpture vultures are well served on the ground floor with the enfilade of sculpture galleries that lead from the Exhibition Road entrance, and the cast courts. The former include works by Rodin such as his notorious *The Age of Bronze*, while the latter are populated with plaster reproductions of famous sculpture and architecture, where the portal from Santiago de Compostella and Trajan's Column jostle for space with reposeful medieval knights and their ladies.

The ground floor is also home to the V&A's ever-popular fashion gallery. Housed in a circular, domed space, this is a veritable pantheon of gorgeous garments, from door-filling court dresses to barely-there flapper dresses and corseted couture by Dior. Downton Abbey fans should look out for the display of Edwardian socialite Heather Firbank's exquisite designer wardrobe, which inspired some of the costumes for the show.

Visitors aged 5-12 might want to take advantage of the museum's award winning 'Back-Packs' (available on Saturdays) to take them through the collections with an innovative mix of jigsaws, stories, and puzzles.

In the warmer months, don't miss the Garden Café, which offers al-fresco light refreshments. Enjoy this sunny spot with its elegant, seasonally updated planting scheme and elliptical pond and see if you can spot the two small plaques commemorating Tycho and Jim, two erstwhile museum dogs.

EXPRESS

PAY HERE

The Cinema Museum

South-East

The Brunel Museum
Museum dedicated to the great engineer
Brunel Engine House, Railway Avenue, Rotherhithe, SE16 4LF •
www.thebrunelmuseum.com • 020 7231 3840 • Rotherhithe LO •
Check website for opening hours • £ • Shop • Café

It took father-and-son team Marc and Isambard Brunel eighteen years to build the world's first under-river tunnel, linking Rotherhithe on the south side of the Thames to Wapping on the north. Located in the original Engine House, this award-winning museum tells the story of their achievement in the face of floods, financial losses and human disaster. 'The Great Bore' as the project was, without apparent irony, called, became known as the 'Eighth wonder of the world' when it opened in 1843. The tunnel paved the way for modern mass urban transportation and is still used today by London Underground – although when it first opened lack of funds meant that the tunnel was initially just used as a novelty underground shopping mall and entertainment venue. Wall displays, models and memorabilia explain the technological triumph of the tunnel as well as revealing the human cost of the endeavour. The lower gallery commemorates Brunel junior's final project, the world's first modern ocean liner, the *Great Eastern*, which was launched just a few hundred yards down the river in 1858.

With its pedimented gables and soaring chimney, this modest brick building is a temple to Victorian self-belief and its characterful museum is similarly aspirational.

The Brunel Museum's imaginative events include walks, talks and performances, some of which take place in the tunnel's atmospheric underground shaft, which boasts a superb acoustic. The rooftop community food garden has also become a hot destination, hosting cocktail evenings during the summer. Elsewhere in the award-winning gardens, visitors can take their ease on benches that have been modelled on Isambard's most iconic bridges.

The Cinema Museum
A living tribute to the history of cinema
The Master's House, 2 Dugard Way, SE11 4TH ● 020 7840 2200 ●
www.cinemamuseum.org.uk ● Elephant & Castle LU ● Admission by
guided tour only ● £

Appropriately housed in the workhouse building that once
sheltered the impoverished young Charlie Chaplin, this
characterful museum is a paean to the days when 'going to the
pictures' truly was a national pastime. The museum, co-founded
by former projectionist and visionary collector Ronald Grant,
embraces all aspects of the cinema from usherettes' uniforms,
lobby cards and posters to swirly-patterned carpets, illuminated
signs and hulking projectors.

The advent of digital projection and the dead hand of the
modern multiplex makes this collection a vitally important record
of the way we once consumed the defining art form of the 20th
century – in sumptuous 'picture palaces', surrounded by a fug
of cigarette smoke, in thrall to the silver screen. A beautifully
preserved art deco screening room, furnished with 36 salvaged
vintage cinema seats, regularly shows material from the film
archive and the museum also hosts film related events, lectures,
and interviews.

The Cinema Museum is not just a museum, but a living tribute
to the history of cinema. It's a place where film enthusiasts can
come together, share their passion, and experience the magic of
the silver screen.

The Crossness Engines
Grand Victorian pumping station
The Old Works, Crossness STW, Bazalgette Way, SE2 9AQ •
020 8311 3711 • www.crossness.org.uk • Abbey Wood Rail •
Admission on open days and by guided tour • £££ • Shop

You name it – somewhere, somehow there's a museum about it. This Victorian sewage pumping station, built by Sir Joseph Bazalgette in response to 'the Great Stink' of 1858, is no exception. Part of the vast sewer system that brought sanitation to London in the last century, the works contain four massive beam engines, capable in their day of raising 6,237 litres of effluent at a stroke. One of these monsters has been restored by a team of dedicated volunteers and can be seen 'in steam' about six times a year. The building itself is a rare example of a Grade I listed industrial site and features some notably colourful and exuberant Romanesque style cast-iron work. Since the completion of a £2.7 million investment the site offers car parking, a café and a much enhanced exhibition space.

The Crystal Palace Museum
Museum dedicated to the great Crystal Palace
Anerley Hill, Upper Norwood, SE19 2BA • 07434 975 582
• www.crystalpalacemuseum.org.uk • Crystal Palace Rail
• Sun 11.00-16.00 • Free • Shop

Designed by Joseph Paxton, the Crystal Palace hosted the 1851 Great Exhibition in Hyde Park before being relocated to Sydenham in 1852. Here it was surrounded by new landscaped gardens where it provided a vast, glassy backdrop to fun fairs, cycle racing and football cup finals, as well as housing a 'national centre for the education and enjoyment of the people', before it burnt down in 1936. Dedicated to keeping its flame (as it were) alive, this museum is situated in the last surviving building constructed by the Crystal Palace Company, a lecture room built in around 1880. Remnants from the building as well as scale models, photos and artefacts associated with Paxton's iconic creation tell the story of this glorified greenhouse.

Cutty Sark
Britain's only surviving clipper ship
Cutty Sark, King William Walk, Greenwich, SE10 9HT • 020 8858 4422 • www.rmg.co.uk/cuttysark • Cutty Sark DLR • Daily 10.00-17.00 • £££ • Shop • Café

Launched in 1869, *Cutty Sark* is the last surviving tea clipper. In her ocean-going days this famously elegant merchant vessel broke records, weathered storms, dodged icebergs and sailed over a million nautical miles before finding permanent residence in Greenwich in the 1950s. In May 2007 the *Cutty Sark* suffered a major fire, but this resilient lady rose from the ashes with the aid of a complex £50 million conservation project. *Cutty Sark* re-opened in 2012, and now sits in a raised position in a glass-covered dry dock where visitors can walk beneath her and admire her sleek copper clad hull at close quarters

Deep in the hold, where once 10,000 tea chests would have been stowed, displays tell the story of the tea trade. There's also room here for a small theatre, which has hosted a surprising variety of comedy stars. The 'tween deck focuses on *Cutty Sark's* eventful career as tea clipper, wool vessel and Portuguese 'tramper', introducing some of the 682 men who served aboard her. Among them was her last master, Captain Woodget who, between watches, found time to breed prize-winning collie dogs, take up roller skating and learn to ride a bicycle.

On the upper deck everything is ship shape, just as Captain Woodget would have expected, with scrubbed wooden deck, gleaming brassware, pristine winding gear and neatly coiled ropes.

A much-loved feature of pre-conservation *Cutty Sark*, the Long John Silver Collection of Merchant Navy figureheads, now convenes at one end of the dry berth. This colourful, slightly eerie, rogue's gallery dates mainly from the 19th century and includes historic figures such as Florence Nightingale, Gladstone and Disraeli, all of whom are overseen by Nannie, the formidable witch who serves as *Cutty Sark's* figurehead.

Dulwich Picture Gallery
The world's oldest purpose-built public art gallery
Gallery Road, SE21 7AD • 020 8693 5254
• www.dulwichpicturegallery.org.uk • North Dulwich Rail
• Tue-Sun 10.00-17.00 • £££ • Shop • Café

Tucked away in a pleasant backwater, the gallery's small but perfectly-formed collection of Old Master paintings is a delight. Arranged by school, the display has been described as a progression from the beer drinkers (Northern European artists) to the wine drinkers (the French, Spanish and Italian schools). A quick glance around the walls reveals a fair smattering of milk drinkers too – as in Rubens' voluptuous *Venus, Mars and Cupid*.

Rembrandt's *Girl at a window* is perhaps the gallery's most famous work and in days gone by was the one most copied by art students; today that honour goes to Poussin, who is represented by seven superlative paintings. The gallery is full of familiar faces and names – Murillo's *The Flower Girl*, Joshua Reynold's bespectacled self-portrait, and Gainsborough's double portrait of beautiful chanteuses, the Linley sisters.

Concise, entertaining wall labels accompany the paintings and for those visiting with children, there are gallery trails to pick up or download in advance, and pencils and paper to use on arrival. The permanent collection is supplemented with exciting touring shows and have featured M.K. Čiurlionis (one of Lithuania's best loved artists), Tove Jannson and Helen Frankenthaler.

The gallery's distinctive building was designed by Sir John Soane and is the world's oldest purpose-built public gallery and inspiration behind Sir Giles Gilbert Scott's design for the red telephone box in the 1920s. The gallery also includes a built-in mausoleum, where the mortal remains of the three founders reside to this day.

The café housed in the elegant bronze and glass 'cloister' extension serves light refreshments. While you're sipping, look out for Peter Randall-Page's *Walking the Dog*, the gallery's first piece of contemporary sculpture, gifted to celebrate its bicentenary in 2011.

Eltham Palace & Gardens

Medieval palace with stunning Art Deco interiors

Courtyard, Eltham, SE9 5QE • 0370 333 1181 • www.english-heritage.org.uk • Eltham Rail • Check website for opening hours • £££• Shop • Café

A medieval royal palace with a twist. The twist being the 1930s house with stunning Art Deco interiors that are incorporated into the ruins of what was once Henry VIII's childhood home. Wealthy couple Stephen and Virginia Courtauld commissioned the house and they kitted it out in luxurious style. Although most of the original artworks and furniture are no longer in place, the house has been restored to its Jazz Age opulence with replica furniture and an Art Deco colour scheme.

The Dining Room features marquetry panels of Italian and Scandinavian scenes (guarded by a pair of bellicose marquetry sentries), the latter with a series of black and silver doors depicting animals from London Zoo. Virginia Courtauld's onyx and gold mosaic bathroom is another essay in the Hollywood style, presided over by a classical statue of *Psyche*. In a bold juxtaposition of ancient and modern, the Great Hall of the medieval palace was rescued from picturesque decay to become the Courtaulds' Music Room. The relentless luxury even extended to the living quarters of Mah-Jongg, the Courtauld's pet lemur who, when not travelling around the world with his owners in their yacht, had use of a roomy heated cage, hand-painted with a tropical jungle scene.

Visitors can also view the billiard room, a wartime air raid shelter and the 'map room', from where the Courtauld's secretary organized the couple's travels. Discovered under numerous layers of wallpaper, the original maps that decorate the walls of this room have been uncovered and conserved. Entrance now includes a free multimedia guide. The palace's 19 acres of gardens have been restored to their 1930s elegance and are perfect for a post-cream tea stroll. Admire the stunning herbaceous border and restored rock garden and see if you can spot the rogue goldfish among the monster carp in the moat.

The Fan Museum
Museum dedicated to the fan
12 Crooms Hill, Greenwich, SE10 8ER • 020 8305 1441
• www.thefanmuseum.org.uk • Cutty Sark DLR • Wed-Sat 11.00-17.00 • £ • Shop

Set in two beautifully restored Georgian houses, this dainty museum oozes gentility from every pore – from its tasteful décor and charming volunteer staff to its award-winning lavatories, and of course, its specialist subject matter.

The permanent display on the ground floor features some pretty, painted fan leaves, including a rare 17th-century example depicting a royal birthday party at the court of King Louis XIV, but the history and art of fan-making are also explored. The fans themselves are crafted with an amazing range of materials, from elaborately carved tortoiseshell, ivory and mother of pearl to Welsh slate. High-profile recent acquisitions include a fan leaf painted with a landscape by Gauguin and one by Sickert featuring a music hall scene.

Regularly changing exhibitions are held in the upstairs gallery and showcase fans from the museum's 4,000 strong collection, exploring decorative and historic themes; previous shows have included fans of the Belle Epoque, advertising fans and Chinese export fans. In 2023 the museum curated an exhibition of fans in the context of coronations and celebrations to coincide with the crowning of King Charles. The museum also runs fan-making workshops and can even design and make fans to order for special occasions.

Fans appear in a variety of guises in the imaginatively stocked museum shop. Fan fare on offer includes specially commissioned jewellery, as well as greetings cards, toiletries, tea cosies, specialist publications and of course a variety of fans.

The Fashion and Textile Museum
Colourful museum dedicated to the history of fashion
79-85 Bermondsey Street, SE1 3XF • 020 7407 8664 • www.
fashiontextilemuseum.org • London Bridge LU • Tue-Sun 11.00-
18.00 • £ • Shop • Café

With its shocking pink and custard yellow façade, the FTM (designed by Mexican architect Ricardo Legorreta), is a vibrant landmark in this increasingly hip part of town. The museum originally opened in 2003 and was the brainchild of flamboyant fashion designer Zandra Rhodes (who was clearly ahead of the curve when it came to locating the museum). It was re-inaugurated in 2008, as part of Newham College, and hosts a programme of changing exhibitions exploring fashion, style and couture. Visitors can expect to see anything from traditional hand-crafted textiles to cutting-edge digital prints and innovative sustainable materials. The exhibitions are accompanied by informative displays and interactive elements, making them engaging and accessible to visitors of all ages and levels of knowledge.

The museum's permanent collection features a diverse range of textiles and garments from the 1950s to the present day, including pieces by renowned designers such as Christian Dior, Mary Quant, and Vivienne Westwood. Keeping a strong focus on fashion and style from the post-war period, workshops and master classes offer experimentation with couture. Through the lens of fashion and textiles many subjects are encountered anew like in their shows 'Andy Warhol: The Textiles' and 'The Fabric of Democracy', which explored printed propaganda textiles over more than two centuries, from the French Revolution to Brexit.

Visitors looking for style inspiration need look no further than the museum shop, which stocks a well-edited range of fashion and design books, stylish sewing patterns and notions, as well as contemporary jewellery and accessories. The bustling café serves award-winning coffee and is a convivial place for a post-exhibition nosh and natter.

Gasworks

Gallery promoting new artists

155 Vauxhall Street, SE11 5RH • 020 7587 5202 • www.
gasworks.org.uk • Oval LU • Wed-Sun 12.00-18.00 • Free • Shop

This not-for-profit contemporary gallery works at the intersection of British and international practices and debates. As well as running artist residencies and offering a community outreach programme, Gasworks holds three exhibitions a year with a focus on commissioning new work by emerging or under-represented local and international artists. A Gasworks exhibition is often the artist's first major exhibition in the UK, making this a great destination for keeping ahead of the contemporary art curve. Open Studio days are held four times a year, offering the chance for visitors to meet the current artists in residence and see their work in progress, and you can also pick up art publications, and limited edition artist prints and gifts in the shop.

Goldsmiths Centre for Contemporary Art

From swimming pool to contemporary cool

St James's, SE14 6AD • 020 8228 5969 • www.goldsmithscca.art
• New Cross LO • Wed-Sun 12.00-18.00 • Free • Café

This site has had many lives: first as a bathhouse in the Victorian era, then as a dancehall and a wrestling venue and lastly as a swimming pool. Its most recent incarnation (and we hope its last) is the architecturally celebrated Goldsmiths CCA, renovated by Turner Prize winning collective *Assemble*. They have retained elements of the building's past while creating eight distinct gallery spaces, including a rooftop room that incorporates the cast-iron tanks from its time as a swimming pool.

With alumni including Steve McQueen, Damien Hirst and Bridget Riley, Goldsmiths is at the centre of contemporary art and this is reflected in their busy exhibition schedule. When visiting the gallery you can take the opportunity to see the current students' working next door.

Hannah Barry Gallery
Cutting-edge Peckham gallery
4 Holly Grove, SE15 5DF • 020 7732 5453 • www.hannahbarry.
com • Peckham Rye LO • Wed-Sat 11.00-18.00 • Free

Gallerist Hannah Barry is one of the movers and shakers behind *Bold Tendencies*, a not-for-profit sculpture project that turns a disused multi-storey car park in Peckham into a cultural hub over the summer months. Her gallery on Holly Grove, Hannah Barry Gallery, founded in 2008, showcases an interesting roster of young artists, including Mohammed Qasim Ashfaq, George Rouy, and Marie Jacotey. The space itself is a former commercial building, and the gallery has maintained its industrial aesthetic while also creating a welcoming and accessible environment for visitors.

At Hannah Barry Gallery, less really is better. With two large spaces over two floors, the gallery condenses the best, brightest and youngest of the contemporary art world with a joie de vivre. And their recent exhibition 'Raw Nerves' was no exception, where sculptures playfully explored the visual and psychological impacts of uncertainty in our modern world. Their fresh and fascinating displays are paired with approachable staff who are always at hand if you have any questions about the art being shown, whether practical or philosophical.

This is no ordinary white cube, as we see in its red panels and graffiti-covered frame – it is part of the city's fabric. The gallery stands as a testament to the creative buzz of this part of town and the wealth of young talent currently working in the city. Even if Peckham isn't usual stomping ground, there's no excuse not to come visit the gallery along with this vibrant area.

The Horniman Museum & Gardens
South London's own Natural History Museum
100 London Road, Forest Hill, SE23 3PQ • 020 8699 1872
• www.horniman.ac.uk • Forest Hill Rail• Daily 10.00-17.30
• Free • Shop • Café

Although firmly rooted in its South London community, the Horniman is much more than a local museum. Boasting a collection of over 350,000 objects, displays include natural history, anthropology and a vast collection of musical instruments. The museum revels in this diversity – and its enthusiasm is infectious.

The museum's in-house aquarium showcases a variety of endangered watery habitats, with the emphasis on conservation. Visitors can follow the journey of a river upstream from mouth to source, peer into the dark waters of a flooded forest pool or wonder at the brilliance and fragility of a coral reef. In these aquatic stage sets the fish – flamboyantly costumed clown fish and stately seahorses – are consummate performers and usually have a captive audience.

A veritable menagerie of stuffed animals populates the Natural History Gallery, centred around an enormous, somewhat elderly walrus. Charmingly retro displays explore topics such as fossils, evolution and adaptation, as well as Forest Hill's own flora and fauna, making the Horniman a well-structured, local alternative to the Natural History Museum.

The Horniman is also the home of Britain's first permanent gallery dedicated to African cultures and the African-influenced cultures of the Caribbean and Brazil. The World Gallery displays over 3,000 objects from around the world, exploring the fundamental question of what it means to be human. Through vibrant and thought-provoking displays, the gallery showcases historic and contemporary objects from all five inhabited continents to show the many ways in which people live. To complement this there is a changing exhibition space on the balcony gallery and there is a further gallery that displays more extensive temporary exhibitions.

The Horniman has gained considerable praise for its recent return of Benin Bronzes and there has been some attempt to reassess the history of acquisition by the museum's founder, Victorian tea tycoon Frederick Horniman. The Centenary Gallery that formerly concentrated on Horniman's legacy has now been transformed into a contemporary art space offering a changing programme of events and exhibitions. Visitors can still handle some 4,000 objects from the museum's amazing collections in the 'Hands-On Base', which is open on an occasional basis (see website for details). The Music Gallery also promises lots of hands-on action with the chance to play a selection of instruments, from an African mbira to 'paddle panpipes' (played with a pair of flip-flops!). Thanks to interactive computers, visitors can also hear what some of the other instruments in this 2,000-strong collection sound like.

The Nature Base is an interactive exploration area kitted out with a bee hive and microscopes. It also features a butterfly house where you can get up close to hundreds of them in a tropical indoor garden, just ensure you book tickets for this in advance as it is very popular.

The Horniman's 16 acres of well-tended gardens include an interactive Sound Garden with outdoor instruments, and display gardens that reflect the themes of the museum's collections. The Animal Walk offers visitors the chance to encounter living natural history specimens such as alpacas, goats, rabbits and chickens.

After enjoying all that the museum has to offer it might well be time for a coffee break. At the Horniman Café you can sit in their gorgeous conservatory overlooking the luscious surrounds and tuck into any number of the treats on offer.

A family-friendly vibe and sweeping views across London and the South Downs combine to make the Horniman gardens a favourite picnic destination in the summer – and a great all round day out.

Migration Museum
The history of immigration
Lewisham Shopping Centre, SE13 7HB • 020 3488 4508 • www.
migrationmuseum.org • Lewisham DLR • Wed-Sat 11.00-17.30,
Sun 11.00-17.00 • Free

Don't let the backdrop of Lewisham Shopping Centre deter you
– this is one of the most exciting museums to have opened in the
past ten years. Considering over 40% of London's population
were born outside the UK, this museum explores how migration
has not only shaped but helped build Great Britain.

Being situated in Lewisham is no accident, as it is one of the
most culturally diverse London boroughs. At the doorway you are
greeted by blocks of the Berlin Wall graffitied by contemporaries
STIK (Londoner) and Thierry Noir (Berlin based). The two works
are symbolic of the founding mission of the museum to provide a
space for dialogue across division.

As well as being the seat of a lot of well-condensed
information about migration patterns, the museum does a good
job at debunking the puritanical 'image' of Britishness. One trivial
example is how Marmite was created by a Swiss immigrant.

Founded by former immigration minister Barbara Roche,
recent exhibitions have included 'Heart of the Nation: Migration'
and the 'Making of the NHS' and 'We Are All Connected', displaying
works by six Ukrainian artists.

To get an impression of the museum, look at their online
exhibition '100 Images of Migration'. From its foundation, the
museum has prioritised its educational outreach and engagement
with locals. The community spirit of the space is what makes it
so special, and most recently it held a competition open to young
people in Lewisham with the chance to hold their own exhibition.
The outcome was *Material Memories*, co-curated by 10-year-old
Muna, a mixed-media display of family objects (artwork, recordings
and poetry) exploring her Palestinian heritage.

National Maritime Museum

The world's largest maritime museum

Romney Road, SE10 9NF • 020 8858 4422 • www.rmg.co.uk/
national-maritime-museum • Cutty Sark DLR • Daily 10.00-17.00
• Free / £ for temporary exhibitions • Shop • Café

The largest maritime museum in the world, the National Maritime Museum explores 500 years of salt-soaked British history, from the swashbuckling days of Drake and Raleigh through to the work of the polar research vessel RSS *Sir Richard Attenborough* and the British Antarctic Survey.

First opened to the public in 1937, visitors enter the museum via the Sammy Ofer Wing, and past Yinka Shonibare's iconic sculpture *Nelson's Ship in a Bottle*. Also on the first floor, the Voyagers gallery, showcases 200 key objects to illustrate our relationship with the sea.

The museum offers a busy programme of family activities including the opportunity to make maps and recently an all-day event called 'Spirit of Windrush' celebrating the 75th anniversary of the arrival of the famous ship to these shores.

For the art curious, the NMM has the largest collection of William Hodges paintings in the world – the artist who assisted Captain Cook's voyage. Found in the Pacific Encounters gallery, paintings like *Tahiti revisited* are remarkable in being some of the first romantic representations of far-flung lands.

There are some remarkable artifacts to be seen in the NMM collection such as the uniform worn by Nelson at Trafalgar in the gallery dedicated to his life and times: 'Nelson, Navy, Nation'. Another great British hero is featured in the 'Polar Worlds' gallery, where a good deal of Ernest Shackleton's equipment can be seen, its rather basic nature, a testament to the difficulty of Artic exploration in his time. 'The Forgotten Fighters' gallery gives attention to the much neglected Merchant Navy and their role in World War I.

If you're not feeling seasick after your adventures on the high seas, the museum café is a great place to catch your breath and enjoy some refreshment.

Newport Street Gallery

Damien Hirst's gallery

Newport Street, SE11 6AJ • 020 3141 9320 • www.
newportstreetgallery.com • Lambeth North LU • Wed-Sun 10.00-
17.00 • Free • Shop • Restaurant

The arrival of Damien Hirst's personal gallery on Newport Street
in October 2015 catapulted Vauxhall onto the art map. Housed
in a lofty one-time scenery painting workshop and designed by
architects Caruso St John to accommodate six exhibition spaces,
covering some 37,000 square feet, this is one emphatic statement
of intent. Indeed, the building is worth visiting in its own right and
won the 2016 RIBA Stirling Prize.

The gallery presents solo and group exhibitions drawn from the
huge art collection that Hirst has been amassing since the 1980s,
which includes works by Picasso, Francis Bacon and Andy Warhol
as well as pieces by fellow YBAs Gavin Turk and Sarah Lucas. The
inaugural exhibition showcased the work of British abstract painter
John Hoyland but Hirst's 'Murderme Collection' is surprisingly
eclectic and also contains works by indigenous artists from the
Pacific Northwest coast, taxidermy and anatomical models.

It goes without saying that the gallery gets first dibs on Damien
Hirst's frenetic output and acts as his studio. Most recently the gallery
made headlines over *The Currency*, an experiment where 10,000 non-
fungible tokens (NFTs) were matched with 10,000 unique pieces of
art created by Hirst. Collectors could decide between either holding
onto the NFT or trading it for the actual artwork. When the deadline
for the exchange ended, slightly over half chose to retain the physical
artwork. Following this, each of the corresponding 'unwanted'
artworks were set on fire by the artist himself.

The Newport Gallery remains the seat of one of the most
acclaimed (and controversial) living artists and at the cutting edge
of contemporary art. Be sure to peg it on any cultural itinerary of
the capital.

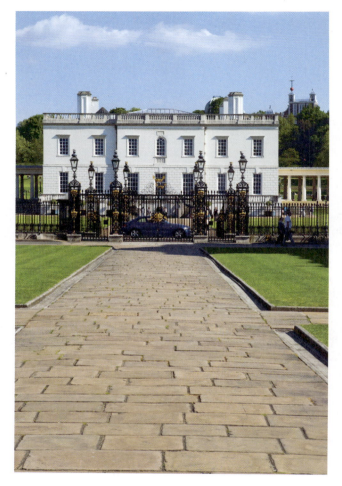

The Queen's House
Royal collection in England's first classical building
Romney Road,Greenwich, SE10 9NF • 020 8858 4422 •
www.rmg.co.uk/queens-house • Cutty Sark DLR • Daily 10.00-
17.00 • Free

Designed by Inigo Jones for James I's wife, Anne of Denmark, this gracious residence holds the double distinction of being the first Classical building in England and the first to boast a cantilevered staircase, the so-called 'Tulip Stairs'. Although it was originally commissioned in 1616, the house was not completed until 1638, by which time the Queen in question was not Anne (who died in 1619) but Henrietta Maria (wife of the ill-fated Charles I).

The Great Hall at the heart of the building is a perfectly proportioned cube with a bold black and white geometrical marble floor. The King's Presence Chamber and its female counterpart, the Queen's Presence Chamber, have been refurbished and hung with paintings depicting historic characters associated with the building's royal past.

The House boasts a fabulous gallery including works by the likes of Reynolds, Hogarth and Turner. The foundation of the Queen's House has long been linked to creative ingenuity and Anne of Denmark was renowned for her support of the arts. Later, during the reign of King Charles I and his consort, Queen Henrietta Maria, the building was converted into a 'House of Pleasures' and adorned with a painted ceiling by Italian artist Orazio Gentileschi and his daughter Artemisia.

Eventually, under the reign of King Charles II, the residence was transformed into an artists studio. In keeping with Anne of Denmark's vision, the house has retained its status as a must-visit for the art curious, with masterpieces like none other than the most famous Queen Elizabeth painting – *The Armada Portrait*. Beyond portraiture they have historic paintings like *Withdrawal from Dunkirk* by Richard Ernst Eurich. As a hidden enclave of British masterworks, this is a must-visit for both art lovers and history buffs.

Ranger's House – The Wernher Collection

Sir Julius Wernher's personal collection

Chesterfield Walk, SE10 8QX • 020 8294 2548 • www.english-heritage.org.uk • Greenwich Rail • Check website for opening hours • ££ • Shop

The gracious interiors of this Georgian villa and former royal residence in Greenwich Park are now home to the Wernher Collection, an opulent assembly of objets d'art put together by self-made millionaire Sir Julius Wernher in the 19th and early 20th centuries. Wernher made a fortune in the South African gold and diamond industries and used his wealth to amass a magnificent and varied collection. Objects on display in the suite of 12 display rooms include bronze statuary, medieval ivories, Old Master pictures, Renaissance jewellery, Sèvres porcelain and majolica ceramics.

The Red Room with its rich ox-blood red walls are hung with Old Masters such as Memling's *Virgin & Child* and *Rest on the Flight into Egypt* by Filippino Lippi, while its displays of Renaissance ivories and medallions are densely packed in 19th-century connoisseur style. No labels intrude on the ambience in this room – if you want to know what you're looking at, you can refer to the smartly bound information booklets. If the Red Room is an exercise in masculine self-expression, the Pink Drawing Room downstairs bespeaks an altogether more feminine sensibility. This was Lady Wernher's domain and it is characterised by deeply pink wallpaper, pretty portraits of 18th-century beauties by the likes of Hoppner, Romney and Reynolds, sugary Sèvres porcelain and curvaceous French furniture.

Reminiscent of the Wallace Collection (see p.112), albeit on a smaller scale, the Wernher Collection offers a similarly revealing insight into what makes a collector tick. Its highlights include the jewellery closet, which contains beautifully crafted Renaissance and Antique pieces, the 'private devotion room' and the Green Silk Room. The collection concludes in The Long Gallery, hung with 17th century French tapestries and overseen at the far end by a dazzling white marble sculpture of angels by Giulio Bergonzoli.

Royal Observatory Greenwich and Peter Harrison Planetarium
Museum at the centre of time and space
Blackheath Avenue, Greenwich, SE10 8XJ • 020 8858 4422 •
www.rmg.co.uk/royal-observatory • Cutty Sark DLR • Daily
10.00-17.00 • £££ • Shop • Café

Straddling the meridian line (at 0 degrees longitude) and home to Greenwich Mean Time, the observatory can claim to be 'the centre of time and space'. Visitors in the Meridian Courtyard photograph each other with one foot in the East, the other in the West. The 'Camera Obscura' is just as fascinating: a revolving panorama of Greenwich projected live onto a table in the middle of the room.

Flamsteed House contains the spartan apartments of the Astronomers Royal and the Octagon Room, a rare example of a domestic interior by Sir Christopher Wren. The display of instruments for measuring time and space include the timepiece that solved the navigators' problem of assessing longitude, and John Harrison's H4 chronometer – reckoned to be the most important timekeeper ever made. Visitors can step inside the dome of the Great Equatorial Telescope (completed in 1893 and one of the largest of its kind in the world) and if you get to the Observatory before 1pm, look out for the Time Ball, which drops at that exact time each day and was used to enable ships on the Thames to set their chronometers.

Over in the Peter Harrison Planetarium, there's a free exhibition 'Exploring Mars', that explains our enduring fascination with our distant neighbour. The displays take visitors from our early visions of Mars with the use of telescopes to contemporary spacecraft travelling millions of miles to explore the planet's surface in the search for life. The displays begin with the very earliest drawings of the planet and end with the stunning images recently taken by the Martian rovers. If all this talk of the red planet whets your appetite, buy a ticket to one of the planetarium's highly enjoyable shows to follow the birth and life of a star and for guidance from a real astronomer on what to see in the sky that night.

South London Gallery
Making art accessible to all
65-67 Peckham Road, SE5 8UH • 020 7703 6120 •
www.southlondongallery.org • Peckham Rye LO • Tue-Sun
11.00-18.00, Wed until 21.00• Free • Shop • Café & Restaurant

Founded over a century ago to 'bring art to the working people of South London', the South London Gallery continues to stage an exciting programme of around seven new art exhibitions every year, together with art and film events, artists' residencies, and a busy education programme. It has hosted internationally-acclaimed artists like Lawrence Weiner and Michael Landy, but remains committed to making art accessible for all with garden trails, play workshops and their youth programme *The Art Assassins*.

The gallery continues to grow, and in 2018 was gifted Peckham Road Fire Station (London's earliest surviving purpose-built fire station) which has become a cultural centre, doubling their space to further expand activities.

The gallery also has wonderful surrounding gardens, the highlight of which is The Orozco Garden that was designed by Mexican artist Gabriel Orozco with the help of horticulturalists from Kew Gardens. The garden uses the vernacular of the gallery's Victorian brickwork and sculpture to make a surprising green environment to explore.

If you're peckish then the on-site café, *South London Louie*, has got you covered, offering up a range of delicious hot and cold drinks, speciality coffee, and a killer weekend brunch. One of the most inviting galleries in London, this is a hopeful space that serves as a reminder of just how vital and versatile our cultural spaces can be.

South-West

Black Cultural Archives
Home to Black British art
1 Windrush Square, SW2 1EF ● 020 3757 8500 ● www.
blackculturalarchives.org ● Brixton LU ● Thu-Sat 10.00-18.00, Sun
12.00-17.00 ● £

It is rare to find a cultural space like Black Cultural Archives that is so enmeshed with its surroundings. Located on Windrush Square, it stands where the first post-war West Indian migrants settled in 1948, establishing Brixton as the heart of London's Afro Caribbean community. In 1998 this square was renamed to mark 50 years since *HMT Empire Windrush* reached our shores.

Entering Black Cultural Archives in such a historically loaded place is a unique experience. Indeed the birth of this archive followed the 1981 Brixton uprising, which was a reaction to the New Cross house fire where 13 young black people tragically died and no one was charged, inspiring the protest cry '13 Dead, Nothing Said!'.

It was in this somber moment that the educationalist and historian Len Garrison felt the void of a space to record, preserve and celebrate the history of people of African descent in Britain and in this to address and oppose the imbalance of power. And so this Grade II listed building became the Black Cultural Archives and has since facilitated discussion, gathering and platforming of art from the African diaspora.

Recent exhibitions include 'Transforming Legacies', an exploration of 21 emerging and established Black British artists spanning 40 years. Celebratory shows are also paired with confrontative shows, like their 2014 inaugural 'Re-imagine: Black Women in Britain', which chronicled 'hidden histories' of influential black figures like Mary Seacole and Jessica Huntley.

In the face of the increasing gentrification of Brixton, the Archives assert that Windrush Square is a place that will continue to be defined by Black history. In a beautiful moment, in 2022, 60 artists gathered there to mark the 40th anniversary of the UK black arts movement. It is this legacy that the Black Cultural Archives continues to commemorate and celebrate.

Dorich House Museum
Studio-home of the sculptor Dora Gordine
67 Kingston Vale, SW15 3RN • 020 8417 5515 • www.
dorichhousemuseum.org.uk • Kingston Rail • Thu-Sat 11.00-17.00
• Free • Café

This unusual modernist house was the studio-home of the sculptor, artist and designer Dora Gordine and her husband, the diplomat turned collector, the Honourable Richard Hare. Designed by the couple in 1936, the house and its collections were acquired by Kingston University after Gordine's death in 1991, and a major restoration programme was undertaken to adapt the house for public use. Returned to its former glory Dorich House holds an important collection of Dora Gordine's sculpture and associated drawings, as well as the collection of Russian Imperial art (including paintings, icons, porcelain, glass, lacquer work, metal work and furniture) amassed by the couple.

Although the house has been dismissed as looking like an 'Eastern European telephone exchange', its uncompromising brick exterior belies its elegant interior. An introductory film plays in the first floor Modelling Studio, and tells the eventful life story of Gordine, and her unstoppable zest for creation (self and otherwise). In the ground floor Plaster Studio, the plaster portraits heads modelled by Gordine include one of the actress Dorothy Tutin. Also on display is a timeline with photographs of some of Gordine's earlier homes. As a serious and successful artist, Gordine made sure that Dorich House really worked for her and the entire first floor was given over entirely to her professional needs, housing a spacious north-facing modelling studio, and a stylish light-filled salon-gallery where she could showcase her work to clients.

Her work fills the room to this day, with pieces such as *Javanese Head* and *The Chinese Philosopher* revealing her long standing interest in Eastern cultures. The couple's more modestly proportioned flat occupies the top floor of the house, with design features such as the sliding Chinese-inspired 'moon' doors and quirky tiled fireplaces adding to the still-tangible bohemian atmosphere of the house.

London Sewing Machine Museum
Largest collection of sewing machines in the world
308 Balham High Road, SW17 7AA • 020 8682 7916 • www.
craftysewer.com • Tooting Bec LU • Open the first Sat of every
month 14.00-17.00 • Free

Balham is not just the 'Gateway to the South' – since July 2000 it
has also been home to this specialist museum. About 550 machines
are lovingly displayed here, the focus being on domestic sewing
machines dating from 1829-1885 and industrial sewing machines
made between 1850-1950. The centrepiece of the display is the
sewing machine made for Queen Victoria's oldest daughter on the
occasion of her wedding, while the oldest machine on show is a rare
Thimmonier wooden sewing machine, treadle operated and still in
working order. Built up over 40 years by one man, Ray Rushton, the
collection is one of the most extensive and best of its kind in the
world and is something of a mecca for sewing enthusiasts, as well as
sewing machine collectors.

Matt's Gallery
Mixed media contemporary gallery
6 Charles Clowes Walk, SW11 7AN • 020 8067 3842 • www.
mattsgallery.org • Nine Elms LU • Wed-Sun 12.00-18.00 • Free
• Shop

Matt's Gallery has moved about a bit over the years but has now found
a permanent site in Nine Elms. The work exhibited here ranges from
painting to video installation and sculpture, all of which is commissioned
specially for the gallery space. Matt's also represents a number of artists
– its 'stable' of well-respected contemporary artists includes Mike
Nelson, Willie Doherty, Nathaniel Mellors, Lucy Gunning and Alison
Turnbull. The bookshop sells the gallery's own publications and there's
also a reading room and archive.

The Museum of Fulham Palace
Former home of the Bishops of London
Bishops Avenue, SW6 6EA • 020 7736 3233 • www.fulhampalace.
org • Putney Bridge LU • Check website for opening hours • Free
• Shop • Café

This beautiful old building – part Tudor, part Georgian and part
Victorian – was once the rural retreat of the Bishops of London. They
were in residence here for over 700 years but the last Bishop left in
1975 and the palace is now home to an excellent little museum telling
the long history of this remarkable site from prehistoric times and
Roman settlement to the present. Although it's notable today for its
relaxed and friendly vibe, the palace has not always been so tranquil;
several of its Bishops came to untimely ends, such as Nicholas Ridley
(burned at the stake in 1555) and William Laud (beheaded in 1645).
The ghost of the Bishop Bonner (died in prison in 1569) is said to
haunt the north rooms of the Tudor courtyard.

More tangible exhibits in the museum take the form of
archaeological remains, a scale model of the palace, a mummified
rat and Bishop Winnington-Ingram's bejewelled mitre and cope.
Benjamin West's pious depictions of Thomas à Becket and Margaret
of Anjou are among the paintings on display.

Several Fulham bishops were keen gardeners and their botanising
legacy lives on today in the palace's 13 acre grounds, which include
many rare trees and a recreated 19th century knot garden. The
historic vinery and part of the walled garden have recently been
restored to productivity. In the gardens look out for *The Bishops'
Tree* by sculptor Andrew Frost, which depicts anti-slavery campaigner
Bishop Porteus, carved into the trunk of a Cedar of Lebanon.

Check their website for the regular schedule of tours to help
make the most of a visit. The stylish but cosy café-bar is a popular
local rendezvous, and does a good line in coffee and cakes.

The Polish Institute and Sikorski Museum
Museum dedicated to Polish history
20 Princes Gate, SW7 1PT • 020 7589 9249 • www.pism.co.uk
• Knightsbridge LU • Tue-Fri 14.00-16.00 • Free

Containing over 10,000 items, this extensive collection relating to this history of Poland is particularly strong on the first half of the 20th century. It is particularly useful for those wanting to know more about Poland and its role in World War II.

Friendly, knowledgeable volunteers guide visitors around – offering a Polish take on events and an interactive experience in the best possible sense of the word. Each branch of the Polish armed forces is represented with memorabilia ranging from battle colours, regimental badges and weapons to photos, documents and personal effects. Exhibits include a Nazi Enigma machine, a submarine map drawn from memory by the crew of the Eagle when their original charts were confiscated, and the uniform in which Poland's war-time leader, General Wladyslaw Sikorski, died. Military paintings and prints line the walls, among them Feliks Topolski's lively portrait of Sikorski and a dramatic depiction of the Battle of Monte Cassino by Edward Mesjasz.

Studio Voltaire
Subversive art in South London
1A Nelsons Row, SW44 7JP • 020 7622 1294 • www.studiovoltaire.
org • Clapham Common LU • Wed-Sat 10.00-18.00 • Free • Shop
& Café

Housed in a converted Victorian chapel, Studio Voltaire features public toilets you can't use and artwork you can sit on – if you're intrigued by this subverted space, read on.

Studio Voltaire is a gallery where no small detail is overlooked: from the entrance to the café, you will be positively floating on a cloud. Ushered in by Anthea Hamilton's spectacular *The Garden*, which forms the entrance to the gallery, the precedent is set. The project was inspired by the vernacular gardens of South London, and features a combination of ornamental flowers, shrubs and edible plants. It's a beautiful place to sit and recalibrate with its fountain and a tiled walkway. Nicholas Byrne's gate for the garden is a work of art in itself and will serve as a second entrance from the south.

This spectacular installation reflects the guiding ethos of the gallery – one of community, reciprocity and accessibility. Indeed, the gallery has built its reputation on showcasing the work of emerging and established artists and has a strong focus on supporting and promoting diversity within the art world. One thing's for certain, this gallery is on the up.

Specializing in installation art, the gallery has a reputation for presenting challenging and experimental work. Nothing reflects this better than their other permanent exhibit *The Institute For The Magical Effect Of Actually Giving A Shit (a note to our future self)*, which uses the context of public toilets to give a tongue-in-cheek institutional critique.

The gallery also has a small shop selling artist editions, books, and other merchandise, as well as an outstanding on-site eatery called Juliet's Café. It features a seasonal menu inspired by the garden, as well as incredible specialty coffee. It's definitely worth ending your visit with a culinary high.

White Cube
The white cube

144-152 Bermondsey Street, SE1 3TQ • 020 7930 5373 • www. whitecube.com • London Bridge LU/Rail • Tue-Sat 10.00-18.00, Sun 12.00-18.00 • Free • Shop

At its inception, this ex-warehouse was the largest commercial gallery in Europe at 5,400 square metres, earmarked by gallerist Jay Jopling as his empire's flagship. The space features three exhibition halls, a 60-seat auditorium for films & lectures plus a shop for esoteric art books. The gallery's design, with its soaring ceilings and clean lines, creates an ethereal atmosphere to view the art on display.

Their recent exhibition 'Once Upon a Time' by Imi Knoebel was quintessentially White Cube, curated by the artist and signalling a radical ever-changing engagement with non-representational art. The exhibition incorporated a narrative component in looking back on his prolific career. White Cube is a perfect place to promote the cult of the artist and Knoebel fully indulged, beginning with an account of his hitchhike to Dusseldorf to ask Joseph Beuys for studio space.

The spectrum of artists exhibited makes White Cube the place to see contemporary conceptual art, frequently showing household British names like Damien Hirst, Tracy Emin and Gilbert & George. Today, the White Cube is one of the most influential contemporary art galleries in the world, with a reputation for showcasing some of the most cutting-edge and provocative contemporary art. The gallery has now expanded beyond London, with locations across the world including Hong Kong, New York City and Paris. Nevertheless, this Bermondsey gallery remains at the centre of the contemporary art world.

Wimbledon Windmill Museum

The Wimbledon Lawn Tennis Museum
History behind the world's oldest tennis tournament
Museum Building, The All England Lawn Tennis Club, Church Road,
SW19 5AG • 020 8946 2244 • www.wimbledon.com
• Wimbledon LU • Daily 10.00-17.00 • ££• Shop • Café
It's hard to believe it now, but lawn tennis was once just a glorified
garden party game, rejoicing in the preposterous brand name of
Sphairistiké. This museum, based at the famous All England Lawn
Tennis Club, follows the development of the sport from its monastic
origins to genteel Edwardian pastime to mega-bucks international
industry – all thanks to the invention of the lawn mower and the
bouncy rubber ball. Naturally the museum also celebrates the unique
sporting event that is the Wimbledon Championships and displays
are top-notch with plenty to enjoy, whether you're a die-hard tennis
nut or a casual armchair aficionado.

Wimbledon Windmill Museum
Museum in a historic windmill
Windmill Road, Wimbledon Common, SW19 5NR • 020 8947
2825 • www.wimbledonwindmill.org.uk • Southfields LU
• Sat 14.00-17.00, Sun 11.00-17.00 • Free • Shop • Café
What better place to tell the story of windmills and windmilling than in
a windmill itself? This particular mill was built in 1817 but converted
to residential use in 1864. Its sails have since been restored and the
building houses a display containing a beautifully detailed wooden
model of the windmill in its heyday, original milling technology and
antique tools, as well as films that recount the development of
windmills from ancient Persia to modern wind farms. Lord Baden-
Powell wrote part of his seminal text *Scouting for Boys* in the Mill
House in 1908, a feat commemorated by a display of Scouting and
Girl Guiding memorabilia. There are hands-on activities for young
millers involving quern stones and grain but if it's all too much of a
grind (pardon the pun), the café is just next door.

575 Wandsworth Road
Where disguising damp became decorative art
575 Wandsworth Road, SW8 3JD • 0344 249 1895 • www.
nationaltrust.org.uk • Clapham Common LU • Admission by guided
tour only, see website for times • ££

Damp is a problem that many homeowners have to contend with but
not many of them respond in the way that Khadambi Asalache did at
575 Wandsworth Road. Faced with a damp patch in the basement,
the Kenyan-born writer, mathematician, architect and British civil
servant disguised the problem by fixing floorboards to the wall
and carving exquisitely detailed fretwork patterns on them. It was
the start of a 20 year interior design makeover that transformed a
modest early 19th-century terraced house on a busy south London
road into a beguiling, and entirely unique, home.

Fretwork decoration covers almost every surface, from kitchen
to bathroom, bedroom to sitting room with motifs and patterns
taking their inspiration from Islamic, African and English influences
– a performance of *Swan Lake* prompted one sequence featuring
ballerinas. A skilled carver and draughtsman, Asalache used reclaimed
pine doors and floorboards to create his masterwork, finding
his modest materials in skips and like an alchemist turning them
into interior design gold (the house has featured in various glossy
magazines). The house stands as its creator left it, with Asalache's
decorations intact and with rooms furnished with his handmade
fretwork furniture and carefully arranged collections of beautiful and
functional objects, including pressed-glass inkwells, pink and copper
English lustreware pottery, postcards and his typewriter.

Asalache died in 2006 and bequeathed 575 Wandsworth Road
to the National Trust who, although the house is entirely unlike
any other National Trust property, accepted it as a work of art in
its own right. The house is much smaller than most National Trust
properties, and is still in fragile condition. Visits are by pre-booked
guided tour only, 6 people at a time, with a maximum of 54 visitors
a week.

Maureen Paley

East

Annka Kultys Gallery
At the forefront of VR art
Unit 9, 472 Hackney Road, E2 9EQ • 07455 561887 • www.
annkakultys.com • Cambridge Heath LO • Wed-Sat 12.00-18.00
• Free

When you stumble onto this congested car park off Hackney Road, you might wonder if you're at the right place. But squint and sandwiched between the garages you'll find the glossier brick and glass façade of Annka Kultys Gallery. Representing a stable of forty artists, the gallery has recently grown into a 'phigital' as well as physical gallery. For those unfamiliar with this jargon, it is essentially a virtual space accessed through Oculus goggles in a portioned off section of the gallery. The benefit of the obscure location is you'll likely have the set to yourself, which can allow you to dizzyingly explore the metaverse.

At the time of writing, they had the 'Web 3.0 Aesthetics: In the future post-hype of NFTs' exhibition, which (thanks to the Oculus goggles) transformed the small room into a Saatchi size institution. Once you get over the embarrassment of fumbling blindly into thin air with the collector in residence, Annka Kultys, eyes on you, it's a mind-bending experience. In the 7 years since its founding, the gallery has become known for its hyperreal and internet art as reflected in the artists they represent like Signe Pierce, Stine Deja, Marc Lee and Ziyang Wu to name a few. With their early exhibitions, such as Molly Soda's 'Comfort Zone' (which featured iPads, iPhones and DM's aplenty), it is no surprise that Annka Kultys next zone to conquer was the metaverse. Although this project is still in its early stages, it's definitely worth watching for more exciting things to come.

Carlos/Ishikawa

Carlos/Ishikawa

Installation space for up-and-coming artists

Unit 4, 88 Mile End Road, E1 4UN • 020 7001 1744 • www. carlosishikawa.com • Stepney Green OU & LU • Wed-Sat 12.00-18.00 • Free

While Stepney Green might be the last place you'd consider to be 'on the cultural map', this gallery is pulling its weight. Ring on the bell to enter this installation space, where you'll probably have the luxury of the gallery to yourself.

Founded in 2011, Carlos/Ishikawa explore structural, socio-cultural, and political issues through the perspectives of diverse artists. Its programme focuses on international artists who often have multi-disciplinary and experimental practices, and aims to challenge the aesthetic conventions of conceptual art. For such a small gallery, Carlos/Ishikawa have done a great deal to platform new and up-and-coming artists, many of whom have gone on to gain recognition internationally.

Chisenhale Gallery

Pioneering East London gallery

64 Chisenhale Road, E3 5QZ • 020 8981 4518 • www. chisenhale.org.uk • Mile End LU • Wed-Sun 12:00-18.00 • Free

Located in a capacious former veneer factory, Chisenhale was set up by artists and runs as a not-for-profit charity. It specialises in work produced by artists having their first major solo exhibitions in London. Up to four new commissions are created every year spanning the domestic and international art scenes, including South African painter Ravelle Pillay and Canadian conceptual artist Lotus Laurie Kang. A solo show at the Chisenhale is a great career stepping stone, and household names such as Rachel Whiteread, Wolfgang Tillmans and Lubiana Himid are all Chisenhale alumni. Exhibitions are accompanied by a lively programme of events, workshop and artists' talks.

Dennis Severs House

Imaginative recreation of a Huguenot home
18 Folgate Street, E1 6BX ● 020 7247 4013 ●
www.dennissevershouse.co.uk ● Liverpool Street LU ● Check
website for opening times ● ££

Dennis Severs House is a real one-off – neither museum nor historic house, it is perhaps best approached as a piece of unique installation art. Created by the late Dennis Severs, an Anglophile Californian who died in 1999, the house is an 18th-century terraced dwelling whose candlelit rooms have been furnished and arranged as a series of atmospheric period 'still-life dramas'. Mr. Severs had strong views about how his creation should be experienced, reminders of which are dotted around the house; visitors are expected to be seen and not heard, and a very museum-like approach to looking but not touching is enforced. Talkative, tactile folk may find these restrictions difficult but restraint is worthwhile – it's hard for the magic to come alive if all you can hear is inane chatter. In the past Mr. Severs would summarily eject visitors who transgressed in this way.

The conceit is that the house is still lived in by a family of Huguenot silk weavers, and going around the house the visitor continually enters rooms they have apparently just left. Subtle recorded sound effects and authentic touches such as brimming bedside chamber pots, unmade beds and food being prepared in the kitchen help create the Marie Celeste effect but the house remains an engagingly leaky time capsule. Period pedants may disapprove but playful anachronisms abound, including poignant reminders of Mr Severs' own occupancy – a NY Yankees baseball jacket draped over the back of a chair, a pair of highly polished English gent's shoes tucked away in a bedroom. The house evokes several time periods, following successive generations of the Jervis family on a journey from genteel Hanoverian prosperity to the Dickensian hard times evoked by the squalid top floor garret. Every Friday they hold a silent candlelit unguided tour to the home which elevates a visit here into an unforgettable sensory experience.

Lychee One

Lychee One

Contemporary gallery offering affordable art

Unit 1, The Gransden Avenue, E8 3QA • 0794 304 4788•
lycheeone.com • London Fields LO • Thu-Sat 12.00-18.00 • Free

Easy to miss but worth tracking down, this emerging exhibition
space focuses on figurative paintings and sculpture, with occasional
provocative performances too, which draws in the nearby art school
crowd. Lychee One describes itself as a meeting point for Eastern
and Western artists bolstered by founder Lian Zhang being the first
mainland Chinese woman to open a contemporary art gallery in
London. Their commercial ventures are particularly approachable
and works on their website start from as little as £5.

Maureen Paley

One of East End's first white cubes

60 Three Colts Lane, E2 6JT • 020 7729 4112 • www.
maureenpaley.com • Bethnal Green LO • Wed-Sun 11.00-18.00

Maureen Paley was one of the first to present contemporary art
in London's East End and has been a pioneer of the current scene,
promoting and showing a diverse range of international artists since
1984. Gallery artists include Turner Prize winners Lawrence Abu
Hamdan, Wolfgang Tillmans and Gillian Wearing, as well as Turner
Prize nominees Rebecca Warren, Liam Gillick, Jane and Louise
Wilson and Hannah Collins.

When it first opened it was initially called Interim Art, but in
2004, as a celebration of its 20th anniversary, it changed its name to
Maureen Paley. The gallery has gone from strength to strength, in
2017 opening a gallery (Morena di Luna) in Hove, East Sussex and in
October 2020 a second space in East London at Studio M.

Museum of the Home
Museum dedicated to domestic life
138 Kingsland Road, E2 8EA ● 020 7739 9893 ● www.
museumofthehome.org.uk ● Hoxton LO ● Tue-Sun 10.00-17.00 ●
Free ● Shop ● Café & Restaurant

Set in 18th-century almshouses, the Museum of the Home (formerly
the Geffrye Museum) is one of London's most charismatic museums.
Visitors get the chance to 'go through the keyhole' to observe the
changing face of English middle-class interior decoration. A walk
through the original buildings takes visitors from the oak-panelled
simplicity of the 17th-century hall to the coolly elegant Georgian
parlour and on to a cluttered Victorian sitting room.

The change in name and modern extension has added to this
narrative with new galleries exploring contemporary domestic
themes and styles. The new spaces use modern media and exhibits
to explore how today's homes are made, ideas of entertainment
in the home and how immigrant communities have settled in a
very different environment. In addition to the permanent displays
is a lively programme of exhibitions covering everything from
photography taken by visitors to local food banks to a multi-screen
video installation exploring the power of music to connect people to
their roots by artist Kadir Karababa.

In December the period rooms are decorated in appropriately
festive fig, while in the summer months the beautifully maintained
walled herb garden and period garden 'rooms' make this a gem of a
museum throughout the year.

The new entrance now faces Hoxton station with an expanded
retail space and café looking out over the traditional gardens and
offering a great place relax after a visit.

Museum of London Docklands
The commercial history of the Thames

1 Warehouse, West India Quay, Hertsmere Road, E14 4AL • 020 7001 9844 • www.museumoflondon.org.uk/docklands • Canary Wharf LU • Daily 10.00-17.00 • Free • Shop • Café

Woefully underused today, the River Thames permeates almost every aspect of London's history. This museum tells the story of London's river, ports and people and their role in shaping the city. An outpost of the Museum of London, the setting for this enterprise couldn't be more appropriate: an early 19th-century warehouse at West India Quay, in the heart of Docklands and in the shadow of the glittering skyscrapers that dominate Canary Wharf.

London was a successful port from the word go and the museum's opening display charts the relentless comings and goings on 'the Thames Highway'. Roman *Londinium* became Anglo Saxon *Lundenwic*, which in turn gave way to the 3rd century port of *Lundenburgh* and not even Boudicca or Viking marauders could dent London's pre-eminence.

'London, Sugar & Slavery' tells the ignoble story of London's part in the slave trade and the sugar industry from the 1700s onwards. 'Sailortown' is a faintly spooky reconstruction of the ramshackle docklands around Wapping, Shadwell and Ratcliffe in the 19th century. Visitors walk down dimly lit cobbled alleyways flanked by a pub, a lodging house and shops dealing in everything from prints to wild animals.

The Mudlarks Gallery on the ground floor lets the under 12s engage in educational fun activities such as 'tipping the clipper', tying nautical knots, and getting to grips with block and tackle technology. The café, at the entrance, has a decent menu from snacks to light meals and also makes a good coffee.

The Museum of the Royal Pharmaceutical Society

Museum dedicated to medicinal drugs

66-68 East Smithfield, E1W 1AW ● 020 7572 2210 ● www.rpharms.com/museum ● Tower Hill LU ● Mon-Fri 09.00-17.00 ● Free

This specialist museum, which relocated to the Royal Pharmaceutical Society's new headquarters in East London, traces the long and fascinating history of medicinal drugs and their use. The museum was initially set up as a collection of pharmaceutical books and manuscripts donated by members of the Society. Over time, the collection expanded to include medical equipment, artefacts, and medicines, reflecting the evolution of pharmacy and the important role of pharmacists in healthcare. The collection is particularly strong on community and retail pharmacy from the 17th century onwards and among its treasures are 'Lambeth delftware' apothecary jars, and glass carboys filled with brightly coloured liquid. The collection also includes more sophisticated dispensary equipment such as antique pill-making machines, a tincture press, and devices for sugar-coating and even silver-coating pills.

But what really sets this museum apart is the interactive exhibits that offer a hands-on experience for visitors. You can try your hand at compounding medicines using traditional methods or explore the history of advertising in medicine through the museum's collection of vintage advertisements.

And proving the old adage that laughter is sometimes the best medicine, the museum displays its sense of humour in a fine collection of 18th and 19th-century medical caricatures poking fun at pharmacists and their patients.

Sutton House

The Ragged School Museum

A lesson in Victorian education

46-50 Copperfield Road, E3 4RR • 020 8980 6405 • www.
raggedschoolmuseum.org.uk • Mile End LU • Check website for
opening hours • Free • Shop

Staffed by enthusiastic volunteers and set in an old canalside
warehouse, this is a charismatic little museum. The site of London's
largest Ragged School, the museum focuses on the work of Dr
Barnardo and education in London but its displays also explore the
lives and history of Eastenders over the last two centuries.

Decked with wooden desks, writing slates and blackboards, the
reconstructed 1880s schoolroom makes an atmospheric centrepiece.
Each year thousands of primary school children take part in the
popular re-enacted 'Victorian' lessons held here. On the first Sunday
of the month lessons are open to everyone, whatever their age. There
is also a reconstructed interior of an Edwardian house.

Sutton House and Breaker's Yard

East London's oldest domestic building

2 and 4 Homerton High Street, E9 6JQ • 020 8986 2264 • www.
nationaltrust.org.uk • Hackney Central LO • Check website for
opening hours • £

Tudor houses aren't exactly ten a penny in the capital these days and
Sutton House is a rare survivor. Built in 1535, it is in fact the oldest
domestic building in the East End and its occupants have included
Henry VIII's Secretary of State, Sir Ralph Sadleir and squatters in
the 1980s. The house still contains early features like linenfold
panelling, stone fireplaces and 17th-century wall paintings. Hinged
panels dotted throughout the house enable visitors to literally peel
back the layers of history and see changes made to the fabric of
the house. The recently added Breaker's Yard is a contemporary
urban oasis featuring a garden and a caravan with a surprising manor
house interior.

The Viktor Wynd Museum
A cabinet (or basement) of curiosity on Cambridge Heath
11 Mare St, E8 4RP • Wed-Fri 15.00-23.00, Sat-Sun 12.00-22.00 •
020 8533 5297 • Cambridge Heath LO • Free • Bar

On a particularly monotonous stretch of Cambridge Heath Road sits Britain's only curiosity museum. Found in the basement of Wynd's bar, there is the unusual bonus of being able to take a cocktail into the exhibition with you. Following from the Renaissance tradition of Wunderkammer, the museum is the brainchild of eccentric and dandy Viktor Wynd – who describes the collection as a sculpture of the inside of his brain.

With objects equally wondrous and grotesque such as moles in jars, shrunken heads, mummified 'mermen', jars of used condoms, well-preserved skeletons of anteaters and 80s erotica, it may come as no surprise that the museum is open to over 18s only. The boundary between real and fictive is blurred, especially in the particularly vulgar instance of a sample of Ms. Winehouse's faecal matter. While these may paint Wynd as someone more interested in the titillating potential of these objects, for the more art curious the museum also holds the largest collection of the surrealist Leonora Carrington's work. If its gruesome contents become a little too much, round off the trip with one of many drinks on offer at the bar, we recommend trying the absinthe from their distillery 'Devil's Botany'. The bar also regularly hosts events like tarot readings and talks with academics involved in the occult. For fellow dandies who want to take their curiosity onto dry land, they even lead 'Gone with the Wynd' expeditions, like a recent one to Papua New Guinea.

Whitechapel Gallery
East London's leading contemporary gallery

77-82 Whitechapel High Street, E1 7QX • 020 7522 7888 • www.whitechapelgallery.org • Tue-Sun 11.00-18.00 • Aldgate East LU • Free / ££ for temporary exhibitions • Shop • Café

Now one of Britain's leading venues for exhibitions of modern and contemporary art, the Whitechapel Gallery opened in 1901 with the aim of bringing major artworks to London's East End. It's certainly achieved that goal with distinction – Picasso's *Guernica* was shown here in 1939 and in the post-war period the Whitechapel has showcased trailblazing artists such as Jackson Pollock, Joseph Beuys and David Hockney. More recently, artists as various as Zadie Xa, Emma Talbot and Simone Fattal have featured. A multi-million-pound development project launched in 2009 and has seen this East London institution double in size with its expansion next door into the former Passmore Edwards Library building, making space for brand new galleries, education rooms and a bustling art bookshop.

The gallery had its 120th anniversary in 2022, and celebrated a history that includes Barbara Hepworth's first retrospective in 1952, and Frida Kahlo's first London exhibition in 1982. That tradition continues with notable recent exhibitions including 'In the Artist's Studio', an exploration of the role of the studio in the lives of artists through history and 'Action, Gesture, Paint: Women Artists and Global Abstraction 1940-70'. The latter, a major exhibition of 150 paintings from 81 international women artists, many of whom had not yet received the recognition they deserved.

If you feel like rounding off your trip in style, the Whitechapel hosts the Townsend restaurant, which serves delicious modern British cuisine in an opulent setting, but if you're just looking for a coffee and a pastry you can find that here too.

William Morris Gallery

Gallery celebrating the founder of the Arts & Crafts Movement
Lloyd Park, Forest Road, E17 4PP • 020 8496 4390
• https://wmgallery.org.uk • Walthamstow Central LU • Tue-Sun
10.00-17.00 • Free • Shop • Café

This award-winning museum celebrates William Morris, the founding father of the Arts and Crafts Movement. A powerhouse of energy and creativity, Morris was also an entrepreneur, poet, translator, Socialist, typographer, and pioneering conservationist. No wonder the cause of his death (in 1896) was given as 'being William Morris and having done more work than most ten men'. Morris lived in this gracious Georgian house from his teens to his early twenties and it's been a gallery devoted to him since 1950. The gallery captures the essence of its subject with just the right blend of scholarship and affection. A series of beautifully re-displayed galleries, guide us through Morris's extraordinary life, from nature-loving childhood and student days at Oxford, to his friendship with the Pre-Raphaelite artists, his enduring legacy as a designer, and his late-flowering career as a typographer and publisher.

Exhibits range from jewel-like stained glass panels to sturdy rustic furniture and Morris' signature nature-themed textiles and wallpapers. Displays reveal some of the luxury commissions that helped make 'Morris & Co' a household name, while 'The Workshop' looks at the labour-intensive craft techniques behind the tapestries, furniture and fabrics that Morris designed, right down to the long-winded processes of making indigo dye.

Morris's influence on the younger generation can be seen in the Arts & Crafts Gallery, which shows pieces by designers such as Voysey and Mackmurdo, and there is also a regularly changing display of paintings and prints by Sir Frank Brangwyn RA, who started his career at Morris & Co. A lively exhibition programme offers thematic takes on Morris's legacy, with recent shows like 'The Legend of King Arthur: A Pre-Raphaelite Love Story'.

Young V&A
Pioneering child-centred curation

Cambridge Heath Road, E2 9PA ● 020 8983 5200 ● www.vam.
ac.uk/moc ● Bethnal Green LU ● Daily 10.00-17.45 ● Free ● Shop
● Café

This East London outpost of the V&A has done a great deal to
shape Bethnal Green into a cultural centre and was the first
public museum in the area when it first opened in 1872. While
for many Londoners a trip to the former Museum of Childhood
will evoke positive memories, it is now moving to a new chapter
in its long history. For its 150th anniversary it is undergoing a
huge refurbishment and in the process will be reborn as the Young
V&A, letting go of its nostalgic roots to be at the forefront of child-
centred museum practices. While still making use of its world-
class collection, it aims to put creation above observation for 0 to
14-year-olds.

Three immersive new galleries – 'Imagine', 'Play' and 'Design'
– will showcase around 2,000 star objects from their collection.
Vibrant multi-sensory interactive galleries will transform and enrich
the building's original Victorian architecture. Welcome additions
include objects displayed at a toddler's height, a wardrobe of
costume materials, and new spaces for hands-on making.

With a fine collection of children's clothes and paraphernalia
like highchairs and prams, the museum also illustrates the social
history of childhood – but few will be able to resist embarking on a
quest to rediscover the toys and games of their youth.

They also host a lively programme of daily drop-in art and
craft, storytelling, games and puppet sessions for children during
term time.

Ham House

Outskirts

Bethlem Museum of the Mind
Charting the history of mental healthcare
Bethlem Royal Hospital, Monks Orchard Road, Beckenham BR3 3BX • 020 3228 4227 • www.museumofthemind.org.uk • Eden Park Rail • Wed-Sat 9.30-17.00 • Free

A museum housed in an NHS psychiatric hospital and dedicated to the history of mental healthcare may not be top of everyone's cultural 'to-do' list, but with one in four of us destined to suffer from a mental problem at some point in our lives, a visit is more relevant than we might care to admit.

Now occupying a former administrative building of Bethlem Royal Hospital, the museum reopened in 2015 after a £4 million refit. The famous statues of *Raving Madness* and *Melancholy Madness* from the gates of the 17th-century incarnation of Bethlem Hospital ('Bedlam') greet visitors as they enter, and pave the way for a non-judgemental display that is rich in artworks, both by well-known artists who suffered mental disorders and by current patients, for whom painting and drawing are important therapies. The collection includes work by Richard Dadd and Jonathan Martin (who tried to burn down York Minster in 1829), as well as Louis Wain, otherwise known as 'the man who drew cats'.

The sensitively curated displays explore the history of the hospital from its foundation in 1247 as well as issues such as diagnosis, treatment and recovery. Exhibits include historic admission records from the hospital, 'before and after' photos of patients by the 19th-century photographer Henry Hering as well as more sobering items in the form of padded cell panels, various forms of restraint, and ECT machines. Handsets enable visitors to listen in on various talking therapies, and there is a touchscreen encyclopedia of mental illness to consult. The exhibition gallery hosts regularly changing temporary exhibitions, enabling the museum to showcase more pieces from its substantial collection of around 1,000 artworks, and other relevant artworks from a range of national and international institutions.

Down House
Charles Darwin's former home
Luxted Road, Down, Kent, BR6 7JT • 01689 859 119
• www.english-heritage.org.uk • Orpington Rail • See website for opening hours • £££ • Shop • Tea room

Originally built as a farmhouse in the 18th century, Down House became the home of scientist Charles Darwin in 1842. It was here that he wrote *On the Origin of Species by Means of Natural Selection*, a controversial book that became one of the defining documents of the Victorian era.

The house remains much as it did in Darwin's day – a family home that was comfortable rather than fashionable, with quirky domestic details such as a wooden slide that whisked Darwin's many children (and even on occasion, his wife) downstairs.

The ground floor rooms, including the great man's book-filled study, have been restored to their 1870s appearance; key exhibits include Darwin's huge journal of his epic five-year voyage on *HMS Beagle* and data-gathering instruments and mementoes from his travels. An interactive exhibition helps visitors get to grips with Darwin's theory of evolution while a multimedia guide offers a tour of Darwin's family rooms.

As well as being extremely pleasant to wander around, the gardens recreate some of Darwin's experiments at Down House, including his research into the reproduction of plants such as orchids and primulas. And if these aren't inspirational enough, visitors can literally follow in Darwin's footsteps by walking along the 'thinking path' he trod daily.

Hall Place and Gardens
Tudor home of the Lord Mayor of London
Bourne Road, Bexley, DA5 1PQ • 020 3045 4088
• www.hallplace.org.uk • Bexley Rail • Visitor centre: Daily 09.30-17.00 / House on selected dates for guided tours • £ • Shop • Café

Now in the tender care of the Bexley Historical Trust, Hall Place was built in 1537 for Sir John Champneys, City merchant and one-time Mayor of London. It's grandeur and original owner make it an interesting south London counterpart to Forty Hall in Enfield, built for a later Lord Mayor, Sir Nicholas Rainton. Architecturally the house falls into two distinct periods – the Tudor hall, with its distinctive checkerboard-patterned walls made of flint and rubble masonry, was joined in the 17th century by the addition of a smart, symmetrically arranged, red brick mansion. The two parts make a very pleasant whole, which is set in 65 hectares of well-tended parkland and formal gardens, complete with a heraldic-themed topiary lawn and display gardens.

Oozing history from every brick, this mayorial status symbol has also in its time served as a boys school and, rather more dashingly, as an Enigma code-breaking station in World War II. Today its historic rooms (which include a capacious Great Hall and minstrels' gallery), also contain a well-presented local history museum charting Bexley from pre-history to the present day. Displays of stone and flint weaponry alongside a woolly mammoth tooth certainly cast suburban Bexley in a different light. By Roman times the area had clearly come up in the world – if the upmarket grave goods on show here are anything to go by. An interactive Tudor gallery looks at everything from Tudor and Stuart fashions to the tribulations of the Reformation. Other permanent displays cover the Victorian and interwar years showcasing objects from the Bexley Museum Collection. The house is open on selected days for guided tours. An excellent café, with a riverside terrace and a Stables Gallery displaying local artists work, complete the visitor experience nicely.

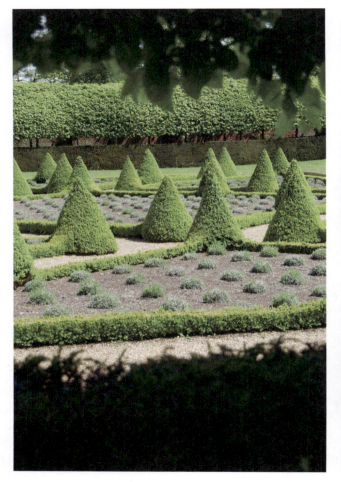

Ham House

Spectacular 17th-century house and garden
Ham, Richmond, TW10 7RS • 020 8940 1950 •
www.nationaltrust.org.uk • Richmond LU • Daily 12.00-16.00 •
££ • Café

Ham House, built in 1610 for Sir Thomas Vavasour, a courtier to James I, and later extended in 1670 by the Duke and Duchess of Lauderdale, is a fascinating historical site that offers visitors a glimpse into the lives of the wealthy in 17th-century England. The imposing, perfectly symmetrical south front of the building makes a bold statement about the power and taste of its occupants, while the opulent interiors are a testament to the wealth and extravagance of the era.

The Duchess of Lauderdale's extravagant redecoration of the house in the 1670s is still evident today, with fine textiles, furniture, and paintings on display that were collected by her over 400 years ago. One of the highlights of the house is the purpose-built library, which was a novelty at the time, and the wooden bathtub and bed in the bathroom, which can be seen on the 'below stairs' tour.

The gardens of Ham House have been restored to their former glory, featuring a wilderness area, a terraced garden, formal lavender parterres, and intriguing outbuildings such as an ice-house, dairy and the earliest known still-house. Visitors can also explore the walled kitchen garden, which grows authentic heritage food crops that supply the refurbished café in the Orangery with fresh produce year-round.

The staff at Ham House are knowledgeable and friendly, always ready to answer questions and provide additional information about the house and its history. Audio guides and guided tours are also available for a more immersive experience. For those feeling brave, ghost tours are held regularly, providing visitors with a chance to see if the Duchess of Lauderdale's ghost really does haunt the house.

Hampton Court Palace
Henry VIII's favourite home
East Molesey, Surrey, KT8 9AU • 0870 752 7777 • www.hrp.org.
uk • Hampton Court Rail • Wed-Sat 10.00-17.30 • ££££ • Cafés

So vast is Henry VIII's Thameside palace that visitors are advised to allow three hours to do it justice, but you could just as easily spend the whole day exploring this iconic chunk of royal real estate. Architecturally speaking, the palace has something of a split personality. On one hand, its expansive red brick sprawl is a stunning example of Tudor architecture with all the crenellations and turrets you'd expect from a royal palace. On the other, it's a stately Baroque masterpiece designed (but never completed) by Christopher Wren. The inside is equally striking with the soaring ceiling of the Chapel Royal to William III's Apartments and onto the 'real' tennis court. Both tennis court and kitchens are still in use to this day. Costumed guides and audio tours help interpret life in the royal household while a permanent exhibition explores the myths surrounding the young Henry VIII and reveals the reality behind them.

The palace still has a few secrets up its sleeve and only recently a long-lost 'chocolate kitchen' was rediscovered. Complete with its original Georgian fixtures and fittings, this sweet-smelling room is where artisans such as Thomas Tosier, chocolate maker to George I, would have prepared his most luxurious concoctions. Another recent development at the Palace has been the Cumberland Art Gallery, a sumptuous setting now home to changing displays of works, by the likes of Rembrandt, Caravaggio and Holbein.

The gardens – all 60 acres of them – are as famous as the palace and include a wilderness, the restored 18th-century Privy Garden, the Great Fountain Garden and the Maze (you may need to allow extra time to negotiate this latter feature). The palace is also home to The Great Vine, which, planted in around 1768, is the oldest and largest known vine in the world. Although there are two cafés, picnickers are welcome and can use any of the benches around the palace courtyards or the gardens.

Kew Palace

Royal palace within Kew Gardens

Royal Botanic Gardens, Kew, TW9 3AA • 0844 482 7777 • www. hrp.org.uk • Kew Gardens LU • Daily 11.00-16.00 • Admission included in entrance to Kew Gardens: £££ • Shop • Café

This red brick, Dutch style 17th-century house was a residence of King George III and his family, and a place of sanctuary for the king during his bouts of mental instability. The construction of the mansion dates back to 1631 when Samuel Fortrey, a prosperous silk merchant from London, commissioned its building as a stylish residence. The smallest royal palace, Kew Palace has been open to the public since 1898 (thank you Queen Victoria) and today visitors can admire its atmospheric restored interiors, such as the smart green and black décor of the Queen's Boudoir ('sulking room') and the Dining Room, where George III would have taken his famously frugal meals. Some rooms, such as the Princesses' bedrooms on the second floor, have been conserved as unrestored architectural palimpsests.

Artefacts on display include the elaborate dolls house furnished by George III's daughters, a startlingly lifelike wax bust of George III, based on a mould made by Madame Tussaud and the chair in which Queen Charlotte died.

The Georgian kitchens – unused since about 1820 – retain many original features and have recently been opened to the public. Entrance is only possible as part of a visit to Kew Gardens, so you'll need to pace yourself if you want to combine horticulture with history.

Kew Gardens is also home to Queen Charlotte's Cottage – an architectural whimsy that provided a scenic spot for the royal family's picnics as well as a convenient place from which to admire the exotic inhabitants of their menagerie. Set in the southwest corner of the Botanic Gardens, the cottage is at its best in springtime, when it is surrounded by a sea of bluebells.

London Museum of Water and Steam
Museum dedicated to London's hydraulic engineering
Green Dragon Lane, Brentford, Middlesex, TW8 0EN • 020 8568 4757 • www.waterandsteam.org.uk • Gunnersbury LU • Sat & Sun 10.00-16.00 • £££ • Shop • Café

Visitors to this excellent museum follow in the footsteps of an earlier pilgrim, one Mr Charles Dickens, who came to admire the Grand Junction Water Works Company's 90-inch engine in 1850. 'What a monster', the novelist wrote of the gargantuan Cornish beam engine – and few would disagree. This impressive piece of Victorian engineering once supplied water to West London and can still be seen in its original cathedral-like pump house, while other lovingly restored steam, diesel and electric engines reside in the Steam Hall and various engine houses. Weekend visitors can see some of these workhorses of the Industrial Revolution 'in steam'. Train buffs young and old can enjoy a ride on the *Wren* type steam locomotive every Sunday from Easter to December.

The Waterworks gallery takes a lively, interactive look at London's water supply, from Roman terracotta conduit pipes to modern desalination processes. A timeline picks out notable watery events in London such as the arrival of the first public water pipe in 1237, and various lethal cholera outbreaks, while scale models show what domestic life was like before and after the advent of safe running water. Meet the heroes of water sanitation such as James Simpson, inventor of the sand filter bed system, or the modern-day flushers, who have the thankless task of clearing obstructions caused by our habit of flushing unsuitable objects down sinks and toilets. The outdoor 'Splash Zone' offers a range of hands-on educational exhibits for younger visitors, who should also keep their eyes peeled for the goldfish that live in one of the engine rooms.

The café serves great coffee and light lunches in the museum's convivial entrance. Outside, there are artists' studios to explore in the old outbuildings while the museum's garden includes a vegetable patch, a wildflower meadow and a pond, as well as the grave of Boulton, the museum's first cat.

Marianne North Gallery
Gallery dedicated to the great botanical artist
Royal Botanic Gardens, Kew, TW9 3AB • 020 8332 5655 • www.
kew.org • Kew Gardens LU • Daily 10.00-17.00 • Admission
included in entrance to Kew Gardens: £££ • Shop • Café

Marianne North was a Victorian artist who specialised in painting
flowers with remarkable single-mindedness. An indefatigable
traveller, Miss North voyaged across the world to paint plants in their
natural habitat, visiting Australia and New Zealand at the suggestion
of Charles Darwin. Her interest in botany stemmed from her father's
acquaintance with Sir Joseph Dalton Hooker, director of Kew.
Although she lacked any formal art training, Miss North was a fast
worker and today some 832 of her distinctive oil paintings can be
seen in the purpose-built gallery she gave to the Botanic Gardens,
whose collection of exotic plants first inspired her.

Described by one commentator as a 'botanical stamp album',
the gallery contains a colourful narrative of flowers, fruits,
landscapes and people taking in harvest scenes in Java, the flora of
Borneo and koalas in New Zealand. When Miss North's request that
her gallery should serve refreshments to visitors was not honoured,
the redoubtable artist pointedly included portraits of tea and coffee
plants above two of the doors.

The gallery – a curious Greek-temple-meets-colonial villa hybrid
– has a floor-to-ceiling display of beautifully conserved paintings.
This is supplemented by an interpretation room and touchscreens,
which allow visitors to see what the views painted by Miss North
look like today – sadly often turned into commercial tourist resorts.
More conventional botanical illustrations can be admired in the
adjoining building, the Shirley Sherwood Gallery (see p.312).

Orleans House Gallery & Stables Gallery
Grand riverside house and gardens
Riverside, Twickenham, TW1 3DJ • 020 8831 6000 • www.
orleanshousegallery.org • Richmond LU • Tue-Sun 10.00-17.00
• Free • Café

With its friendly vibe and excellent café, Orleans House is a popular riverside destination and the gallery adds a cultural dimension, hosting around twelve exhibitions a year, exploring pertinent local subjects and often featuring items from the Borough of Richmond's collection of artworks dating from the 18th century. Exhibitions in the Stables Gallery tend to have a more contemporary focus and there is also a lively programme of arty activities for all ages. Orleans House was once a royal residence (the Duc d'Orléans was exiled here between 1815-17), and its elegant Octagon Room is a small but sweet gem of Baroque architecture, designed by James Gibbs and featuring elaborate stucco work and Hanoverian portraits. The stable block now houses an excellent café.

Osterley Park and House
Tudor manor house and gardens
Jersey Road, Isleworth, Middlesex, TW7 4RD • 020 8232 5050
• www.nationaltrust.org.uk • Osterley LU • Wed-Sun 11.00-15.30
• ££ • Café • Shop

A red brick Tudor manor house built by Sir Thomas Gresham and remodelled inside and out for the upwardly mobile Child family in the 18th century by John Adam. Stunning Georgian interiors include the austere entrance hall of 1767 and the tapestry room, hung with crimson-coloured Boucher medallion tapestries specially commissioned from the Gobelin factory in Paris. Clocking in at 130 feet, the Long Gallery is aptly named and is now hung with an assemblage of 17th and 18th-century Venetian paintings. The house is set in 357 acres of parkland with lakes and mature oak trees. The recently restored pleasure gardens boast a walled vegetable garden, an American garden, a winter garden and, in spring, the bluebell-bordered Long Walk.

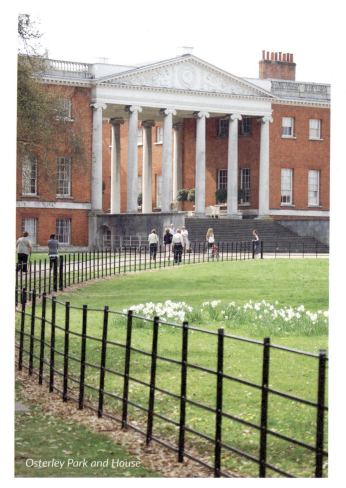

Osterley Park and House

Shirley Sherwood Gallery of Botanical Art

Red House
Only house designed by William Morris
Red House Lane, Bexleyheath, Kent DA6 8JF • 020 8303 6359
• www.nationaltrust.org.uk/red-house • Bexleyheath Rail • Pre-booked tours only from March to Oct

A must for William Morris fans, Red House is the only house to have been created by the great designer and he moved here as a young man in 1860, with his newly wedded wife Jane. Built for Morris by his friend Philip Webb, the house is a romantic essay in medieval-Gothic style, complete with steep tiled roofs, an L-shape layout and, yes, a lot of red brick. The interiors are not fully furnished but the original Arts & Crafts features, together with the odd piece of furniture by Webb and Morris and wall-paintings by Burne-Jones help to compensate. It was at Red House that Morris began to work as a designer and examples of his famous wallpaper designs, like *Trellis* and *Daisy* are also displayed. The surrounding garden was a source of inspiration for Morris and today is something of a green oasis in suburban Bexleyheath, with its lovely wisteria around the house, ancient apple orchard, croquet lawn and a productive vegetable garden.

Shirley Sherwood Gallery of Botanical Art
Botanical art gallery in Kew Gardens
Royal Botanic Gardens, Kew, TW9 3AB • 020 8332 5655 • www.kew.org • Kew Gardens LU • Daily 10.00 17.00 • Admission included in entrance to Kew Gardens: £££

Kew holds one of the world's greatest collections of botanical art numbering around 200,000 works, but until this gallery opened in 2008, had nowhere to display these often fragile works. Designed by architects Walters & Cohen and built next to the Marianne North Gallery, this sleek, purpose-built gallery finally allows the public the chance to see Kew's historic gems, along with pieces from Dr. Sherwood's own impressive collection of contemporary botanical illustrations. Past exhibitions have been themed around flowering bulbs and tubers, fruit and Kew's heritage trees.

Strawberry Hill House & Garden
Gothic revival home of Sir Horace Warpole
Strawberry Hill, 268 Waldegrave Road, Twickenham, TW1 4ST
• 020 8744 1241 • www.strawberryhillhouse.org.uk • Strawberry
Hill Rail • Sun-Wed 11.00-16.00 • ££ / Garden free • Shop • Café

Modern-day visitors to Strawberry Hill follow in the footsteps of their 18th-century forebears who flocked to see the 'little Gothic castle' dreamed up by Horace Walpole, renowned collector, man of letters, and son of Britain's first prime minister Sir Robert Walpole. Friendly room stewards are on hand to answer questions and help with navigation but other than that you're on your own, and free to admire at your own pace the extraordinary creation built by Horace as a summer villa between 1748 and 1790.

Students of architecture know Strawberry Hill as the first and finest example of Gothic revival architecture with its atmospheric interiors, landscaped garden and wedding cake white exterior. The huge collection that Walpole amassed over his life to fill the house was flogged off by a spendthrift descendent in 1842, but long term loans from Dulwich Picture Gallery and eight works from a private collection help to recreate the atmosphere of Strawberry Hill House as it would have been in its heyday.

Always intended as a theatrical experience, the house takes visitors on a journey through the 'gloomth' of the dimly lit entrance hall and the Stygian darkness of the Star Chamber to show-stopping State Rooms such as the Gallery, with its vivid crimson walls and intricate gold papier-mâché tracery ceiling and mirrored alcoves. Room after room exercise their magic, from the medieval-inspired library, to the purple-painted Holbein Chamber, where once hung Cardinal Wolsey's red hat.

Walpole's Bedchamber was where he experienced the dream that inspired the writing of the first Gothic horror novel, *The Castle of Otranto*. There's a copy of the book to read in The Plaid Bedchamber, while in the Dressing Room next door is a display devoted to the private printing press that Walpole set up at Strawberry Hill.

Valence House Museum
Home of the Dagenham Idol
Becontree Avenue, Dagenham, RM8 3HT • 020 8227 2034
• www.valencehousecollections.co.uk • Becontree LU • Tue-Sat
10.00-16.00 • Free • Shop • Café

If you had ever wondered where you might find the oldest depiction of a human figure in Europe, then wonder no more. It is here, in the excellent local history museum that serves the London Borough of Barking and Dagenham. Dating from around 2250 BC, the Dagenham Idol was unearthed in 1922, at around the time that the Borough's famous Becontree Estate, the largest public housing development in the world, was being built. Both the Neolithic figure and the recently restored medieval manor in which it is housed are rare survivors in an area that has played host to prehistoric hunters, Roman settlers, Viking raiders and idealistic urban planners.

At 700 years old, Valence House is a newcomer, but its wonky old rooms provide an atmospheric backdrop to exploring the multi-faceted history of the Borough. Along the way visitors meet some of the Borough's illustrious sons and daughters, from Barking Abbey's feisty Abbesses, to sporting legends such as Bobby Moore and Sir Alf Ramsay and the legendary Dagenham Girl Pipers. Some of the Borough's pastimes and recreational activities can be seen in the screening room that shows vintage films of the area including those made by the Dagenham Co-Operative Film Society from the 1940s onwards. And as if this wasn't enough, the museum is also home to one of the country's finest collections of 'gentry portraiture', depicting local bigwigs, the Fanshawe family, from the Elizabethan era through to the 20th century. Voted one of the 50 best free things to do in London, Valence House also offers a year-round programme of family-friendly events.

Appendix

Archives & Libraries

This listing is not intended to be exhaustive – London's archives and libraries merit a guide in their own right. In addition, many of the museums and galleries listed in this book also have their own research libraries and archives and more information about these can usually be found on the relevant institution's website.

Ashmole Archive
Dept of Classics, King's College London, Strand, WC2R 2LS •
classics@kcl.ac.uk
The Ashmole is a photographic archive of ancient Greek sculpture, which can be viewed by appointment only.

BFI Reuben Library
BFI Southbank, Belvedere Road, SE1 8XT • 020 7255 1444 •
www.bfi.org.uk • Tue-Sat 11.00-19.00
Established in 1934, the library's collection spans the history of the moving image and includes books, journals, press cuttings and digitised materials. Located in the South Bank Centre, it offers open access to its comfortable study areas and a vast archive of books, journals and digital material relating to the moving image. The website is a good first point of call.

Bishopsgate Institute
230 Bishopsgate, EC2M 4QH • 020 7392 9270 •
www.bishopsgate.org.uk • Mon-Fri 10.00-17.00, Wed till 20.00
The Bishopsgate Institute has been providing education services and an extensive library from this Grade II listed building since 1895. The institute holds major collections of books and documents concerning London, Labour and Socialist History, Humanism and political figures. There is also an archive of over 150,000 images of London that are used for a busy programme of exhibitions.

The Bishopsgate Institute

Black Cultural Archives

1 Windrush Square, Brixton, SW2 1EF • 020 3757 8500 •
www.bcaheritage.org.uk • Tue-Sat 10.00-18.00

The Black Cultural Archive is a community-based heritage
organisation and archive that collects, preserves and celebrates the
history and culture of black people in Britain. The archive's purpose-
built Heritage Centre is located in the heart of Brixton and offers a
busy programme of events and classes (see p.247 for full review).

British Library

96 Euston Road, NW1 2DB • 0330 333 1144 • www.bl.uk
• Mon-Thu 9.30-20.00, Fri 9.30-18.00, Sat 9.30-17.00 & Sun
11.00-17.00

The British Library holds the largest collection of books in the
world with access largely restricted to those undertaking academic
research. Those without academic accreditation will still enjoy
visiting the library with a busy programme of lectures, concerts, tours
and exhibitions (see p.122). When visiting the library don't forget
to take a look at the vast six-storey glass tower at the centre of the
building containing King George III's collection of over 65,000 books.

British Library Sound & Vision Archive

96 Euston Road, NW1 2DB • 020 7412 7418 • www.bl.uk/nsa
• By appointment only

One of the largest sound archives in the world with over 3 million
sound recordings. The extensive collection covers music (classical,
popular, world and folk), drama and literature, oral history, wildlife
sounds, dialects and accents. Access to the archive is now restricted
to British Library pass holders and it is advised to contact the archive
with details of what you are looking for before making a visit, so that
material can be prepared in advance.

The British Psychoanalytical Society

Byron House, 112A Shirland Road, W9 2BT • 020 7563 5010
• www.psychoanalysis.org.uk • By appointment only (email:
archives@iopa.org.uk)

The British Psychoanalytical Society Archive holds a wealth of
material on the history of psychoanalysis in Britain and abroad,
reflecting its role in medicine, mental health and wider society. The
Society charges £12 for a daily access pass.

BT Archives

Third Floor, Holborn Telephone Exchange, 268-270 High Holborn,
WC1V 7EE • www.bt.com/archives • Mon-Tue 10.00-16.00 • By
appointment only

BT Archives preserves the historical information of British
Telecommunications plc and its predecessors from the early part of
the 19th century to the present day. The archive contains telephone
directories dating back to 1880, historical records, as well as the
historic photographic, video and film collections of BT and Post
Office Telecommunications.

City of Westminster Archives Centre

10 St Ann's Street, SW1P 2DE • 020 7641 5180 •
www.westminster.gov.uk/libraries • Tue-Thu 10.00-19.00, Fri &
Sat 10.00-17.00

This archive extends over five floors and contains varied collections
relating to the history of Westminster including the business records
for companies such as Liberty, Jaeger and Lobbs as well as theatre
programmes, maps and local government records.

Conway Hall Ethical Society

Conway Hall, 25 Red Lion Square, WC1R 4RL • 020 7061 6747 •
www.conwayhall.org.uk • Fri 10.00-15.00 • By appointment only

Conway Hall houses the country's largest Humanist research library
with over 10,000 books, periodicals and pamphlets.

Courtauld Institute of Art Libraries

Somerset House, Strand, WC2R 0RN• 020 3947 7777 •
www.courtauld.ac.uk • By appointment only

London's pre-eminent centre for the study of history of art has
three libraries. The book library is academic and contains a major
collection of art books, periodical and exhibition catalogues, while
the Witt Library contains some 2 million reproductions of works by
over 70,000 artists. The Conway Library performs a similar service
for architecture and sculpture.

Crafts Council Research Library

44a Pentonville Road, Islington, N1 9BY • 020 7806 2500 • www.
craftscouncil.org.uk • By appointment only

A free-to-browse library containing books, journals and videos
relating to craft technique and practice, funding directories, as well
as exhibition catalogues and Crafts Council research reports.

Great Ormond Street Hospital Archives

Archive Service, Great Ormond Street Hospital for Children,
Great Ormond Street, WC1N 3JH • 020 7405 9200 • www.gosh.
nhs.uk/about-us/our-history/archives • By appointment only

Great Ormond Street Hospital's archive contains documents,
photographs and artefacts spanning the hospital's 160-year history.
It holds an extensive range of material from 1852 onwards, including
correspondence relating to Peter Pan (the rights of which were given
to the hospital by the author Sir JM Barrie).

Lambeth Palace Library

Lambeth Palace Road, SE1 7JU • 020 7898 1400 • www.
lambethpalacelibrary.org • Mon-Fri 9.30-17.00, Thu till 19.30

Founded in 1610 by Archbishop Bancroft, this is one of the oldest
public libraries in Britain. It is the principal library and record office
for the Church of England and contains a vast collection of archives,
books and manuscripts relating to ecclesiastical history.

London Archaeological Archive & Research Centre

Mortimer Wheeler House, 46 Eagle Wharf Road, N1 7ED •
020 7550 9999 • www.mola.org.uk • By appointment only
The LAARC holds information on over 5,000 London sites and archaeological projects from the past 100 years, including records and finds from archaeological digs. It is a fascinating resource but one only available to researchers by appointment.

The London Library

14 St James's Square, SW1Y 4LG • 020 7766 4700 • www.
londonlibrary.co.uk • Mon-Tue 9.30-21.00, Wed-Sat 9.30-17.30
Founded by the historian and essayist Thomas Carlyle in 1841, the London Library has become one of the largest independent subscription libraries in the world with over a million books. Annual membership costs £585 and includes unlimited lending rights and access to over 750 academic journals.

London Metropolitan Archives

40 Northampton Road, EC1R 0HB • 020 7332 3820 • www.
cityoflondon.gov.uk/lma • Mon-Tue & Thu 10.00-16.00; Wed
10.00-19.00
A treasure trove for anyone researching anything about London or Londoners. As county record office for Greater London, the LMA holds records for the GLC and LCC, 900 London parishes, hospitals, business records and family papers. Among the original documents is a copy of the Magna Carta.

Marx Memorial Library

37a Clerkenwell Green, EC1R 0DU • 020 7253 1485 •
www.marx-memorial-library.org • Mon-Thu 11.00-16.00
This independent library is dedicated to all aspects of Marxism, the 'science' of Socialism and the history of working class movements. The library also contains an archive on the Spanish Civil War and an extensive picture library.

The National Archives

Ruskin Avenue, off Mortlake Road, Kew, Surrey, TW9 4DU • 020 8876 3444 • www.nationalarchives.gov.uk • Tue & Thu 9.30-19.00, Wed & Fri-Sat 9.30-17.00

Based in an impressive waterside building in Kew, this is the UK government's official archive and holds 900 years of official records, from the Domesday book to the latest government papers. Records are normally made available to the public when they have been archived for 30 years and can be accessed by anyone over the age of 14 on production of proof of address and identity.

For those researching family history, Kew is now also home to the archive of the Family Records Centre. This is the repository for census returns from 1841-1891, non-conformist records and records of the Prerogative Court of Canterbury, wills and administrations, as well as records of birth, deaths and marriages, dating back to 1837. If you can't make it to Kew, the DocumentsOnline service (www.discovery.nationalarchives.gov.uk) provides access to over a million documents held in the archives.

National Art Library

V & A Museum, Cromwell Road, SW7 2RL • www.vam.ac.uk/nal • Tue-Thu 11.00-17.00

This grand public library is the country's largest reference library for the fine and decorative arts. The library is located within the V & A and can be accessed with the purchase of a reader's ticket.

National Portrait Gallery

Heinz Archive and Library, St Martin's Place, WC2H 0HE • 020 7321 6617 • www.npg.org.uk/research/archive • By appointment only

This archive contains drawings, prints and photographs of British portraits dating from 1400 to the present day.

The Poetry Library

Level 5, Royal Festival Hall, Belvedere Road, South Bank,
SE1 8XX • 020 7921 0943/0664 • www.poetrylibrary.org.uk •
Wed-Sun 12.00-20.00, Tue 12.00-18.00

The most comprehensive and accessible collection of poetry in
Britain, The Poetry Library within the Southbank Centre contains
90,000 items and is still growing. The Arts Council collection
consists mostly of poetry from the UK and Ireland, a large selection
from English-speaking countries worldwide, poetry in translation as
well as poetry by and for children. Audio and video facilities are
available in addition to a large variety of magazines, press cuttings
and downloadable poems. The library is an oasis of calm amid the
noise and bustle of the Royal Festival Hall and offers great views
across the Thames.

RIBA Architecture Study Rooms

V&A Museum, South Kensington, Cromwell Road, SW7 2RL • 020
7307 3708 • www.vam.ac.uk • By appointment only

A partnership between the V&A and the RIBA allowing access
to the RIBA's outstanding collection of architectural drawings
and manuscripts in the RIBA Architecture Study Rooms, housed
alongside the V&A's Prints & Drawings Study Room. The collections
comprise the RIBA's collection of drawings and archive and the
V&A's collection of drawings, photographs and prints.

RIBA British Architectural Library

66 Portland Place, W1B 1AD • 020 7307 3882 •
www.architecture.com • Tue 12.00-19.00, Mon, Wed-Fri
11.00-17.00

The RIBA Library is one of the world's largest archives relating
to architecture and architectural history. Unlike many august
institutions RIBA offer free public access to the library. See also the
RIBA Architecture Drawings and Archives at the V&A (see p. 202).

The Poetry Library

Royal Geographical Society
1 Kensington Gore, SW7 2AR • 020 7591 3000
www.rgs.org • Mon-Fri 10.00-13.00,14.00-17.00 • ££

The Society holds one of the most important geographical collections in the world. The collection includes more than 150,000 books (dating from as far back as 1830), 800 current journal titles, expedition reports (including David Livingstone's), maps and charts, atlases and a picture library holding more than 500,000 images from around the world. If all of this gives you itchy feet the Society provides information on planning expeditions.

The Royal Mail Archive
Freeling House, Phoenix Place, WC1X 0DL • 0300 0300 700•
www.postalmuseum.org • Tue-Wed & Fri 10.00-17.00 and second Saturday of each month, Thu 10.00-19.00

The archive, tucked away near Mount Pleasant sorting office, contains records of the Post Office and Royal Mail from 1636 to the present. The postal staff archive is a useful resource for family history researchers while the collection of British stamps runs from the Penny Black onwards. A small exhibition area holds regularly changing philatelic displays.

The Salvation Army International Heritage Centre
William Booth College, Denmark Hill, SE5 8BQ • 020 7326 7800 •
www.salvationarmy.org.uk/international-heritage-centre • Tue-Fri 9.30-16.00 • By appointment only

The Heritage Centre includes a reference library and archive and is open to researchers by appointment. Among the treasures in the archive are the papers of Sally Army founders William and Catherine Booth, plus a host of SA publications and records from UK local centres.

Wiener Library

29 Russell Square, WC1B 5DP • 020 7636 7247 •
www.wienerholocaustlibrary.org • Mon-Fri 10.00-17.00, Tue till
19.00

Formed in 1933 by a refugee from Nazi Germany, Dr Alfred Wiener,
the Wiener Library is one of the world's most extensive archives on
the Holocaust and Nazi era. The Library's unique collection of over
a million items includes published and unpublished works, press
cuttings, photographs and eyewitness testimony. The library runs a
busy programme of exhibitions and lectures on subjects relating to
Jewish history, Israel, anti-semitism and the Holocaust.

Women's Library

LSE Library, 10 Portugal Steet, WC2A 2HD • 020 7955 7229 •
www.lse.ac.uk • By appointment only

This archive of women's history and reference material is the oldest
and most extensive women's resource in Europe, established in
1926. The collection is now held within the LSE and includes books,
pamphlets, periodicals, press cuttings and archival collections. A
large part of the collection has been digitalised and can now be
viewed online.

London Art Fairs

January

The London Art Fair

Business Design Centre, Islington, N1 0QH •
www.londonartfair.co.uk

This busy art fair brings together over 100 galleries, showcasing the brightest and best in modern British and international contemporary art.

March

The Affordable Art Fair

Battersea Park, SW11 4NJ • www.affordableartfair.com

'Affordable' is a relative term of course, but this hugely popular art fair brings together a range of dealers from across the world showing accessible, reasonably priced art aimed at first-time and younger buyers. Consult the website before setting off on your shopping spree – it's full of sound advice for buying art. They also have an autumn event (see October for further details).

Collect

Somerset House, The Strand, WC2R 1LA •
www.collectfair.org.uk

International art fair for museum-quality contemporary applied art – this is the place to find mouthwateringly beautiful glass, jewellery, metalwork, textiles, woodwork and furniture.

The Other Art Fair

The London Original Print Fair

Somerset House, The Strand, WC2R 1LA •
www.londonoriginalprintfair.com

London's longest running art fair brings together nearly 50 dealers, between them showing the gamut of graphic art from early printmakers like Dürer to contemporary practitioners such as David Hockney. Prints are often an affordable way to buy a big name artist's work and the fair's website contains lots of helpful information about the various print techniques.

The Other Art Fair

The Truman Brewery, 85 Brick Lane, E1 6QR •
www.theotherartfair.com

Artists rather than dealers are the exhibitors here, making this biannual fair the ideal place to buy direct from emerging contemporary artists.

May

Photo London

Somerset House, The Strand, WC2R 1LA • photolondon.org

International photography fair that gathers around 80 specialist galleries from around the world, and combines the retail action with a public programme of events, site specific installations, exhibitions and talks.

September/October

The Goldsmiths' Fair

Goldsmiths' Hall, Foster Lane/Gresham Street, EC2 6BN •
www.thegoldsmiths.co.uk

A magnet for magpies and jewellery lovers, this fair showcases a glittering selection of work by top silver and goldsmith designer-makers. It's a great opportunity to meet the makers in person, and perhaps purchase or commission a piece of wearable art.

The Affordable Art Fair
Battersea Park, SW11 4NJ • www.affordableartfair.com
See March for more details.

Frieze London
Regent's Park, NW1 4NR • www.frieze.com
Founded in 2003, this international contemporary art fair has become a world leader, attracting visitors and column inches in volume. It brings together over 150 handpicked galleries from around the world and places them in the sylvan surrounds of Regent's Park. A carefully curated programme of projects and talks accompanies the fair.

Frieze Masters
Regent's Park, NW1 4HG • www.frieze.com
This runs at the same time as Frieze London but offers 'a contemporary lens on historical art'. The best of art through 6,000 years of history presented by some of the world's leading galleries.

PAD London
Berkeley Square, W1J 5AX • www.pad-fairs.com
Housed in a chic black tent in the heart of Mayfair, this fair focuses on 20th century art, design and decorative arts. Exhibitors are vetted and include an international rosta of top galleries.

January/May/October

The Decorative Antiques and Textiles Fair
Battersea Park, SW11 4NJ • www.decorativefair.com
Thrice yearly fair, held in a marquee in Battersea Park, and dedicated to 'antiques for interiors' and 20th century design. Exhibitors tend to show their work in room-sets so this is a great place to pick up ideas for your home.

Eltham Palace

General Index

Subject Index

The Garden Museum

Image Credits

Staircase © Handel & Hendrix in London, p.4 © Wallace Collection, p.6 © Alison Jacques, p.9 © Metro Publications, p.10 © Metro Publications, p.13 The Great Court, British Museum © Stephen Millar, p.14 © British Museum, p.16 © The Cartoon Museum, p.19 © The Charterhouse, p.20 © Churchill War Rooms, p.23 © Colnaghi, p.25 © Courtauld Gallery, p.27 © David Zwirner, p.28 © The Faraday Museum, p.31 © Florence Nightingale Museum, p.32 © Foundling Museum, p.35 © Gagosian, p.36 © Metro Publications, p.39 © Grant Museum of Zoology, p.41
© Hamiltons Gallery, p.42 © Handel and Hendrix in London, p.45 Install view of 'Günther Förg. Tupfenbilder' at Hauser & Wirth London, Courtesy the Günther Förg estate and Hauser & Wirth, p.46 © Metro Publications, p.49 © HMS Belfast, Imperial War Museum, p.50 © Household Cavalry Museum, p.53 Hunterian Museum © Hufton + Crow, p.54 &57 © Imperial War Museum, p.58 Institute of Contemporary Art, Photo: Linda Wilkins, p.61 The Jewel Tower, © English Heritage, p.62 © Dr Johnson's House, p.65 © Kirkaldy Testing Museum, p.66 © Metro Publications, p.69 & 70 © London Transport Museum, p.73 © Marlborough Galleries, p.74 © Metro Publications, p.77 Library and Museum of Freemasonry © Stephen Millar, p.78 © The National Gallery, p.81 Vincent van Gogh, *Sunflowers* © The National Gallery, p.82 © Colin Streater/National Portrait Gallery, p.85 © National Portrait Gallery, p. 86 © The Old Operating Theatre Museum& Herb Garret, p. 89 Courtesy Pace Gallery, London © Giddeon Appah, photo Damian Griffiths, p.90 Courtesy Photographers' Gallery © Luke Hayes, p.93 © The Postal Museum, p.94 Courtesy Rebecca Hossack Gallery © Lubka Gangarova, p.97 Royal Academy of Arts, p.98 Sir John Soane's Museum © Martin Charles, p.101 © Sprüth Magers / photo Timo Ohler, p.102 © Spencer House, p.105 & 106 © Metro Publications, p.109 © Metro Publications, p.110 © Two Temple Place, p.113 © Wallace Collection, p.114 Courtesy of White Cube © Ollie Hammick, p.117 © 180 Studios, 180 The Strand, p. 118 © Estorick Collection of Modern Italian Art, p.121 © Ben Uri Gallery & Museum, p.122 © British Library, p.125 © Burgh House, p.127 © Camden Art Centre, p. 129 © Estorick Collection of Modern Italian Art, p.130 Fenton House © National Trust, p.133 © Freud Museum London, p.134 © The Jewish Museum, p.137 © Keats House, p.138 Kenwood House © English Heritage, p.141 Courtesy Lisson Gallery © Julian Opie, p.142 © The London Canal Museum, p.145 © Queer Britain, p.146 Royal Airforce Museum, p.149 © Metro Publications, p.150 Adam Shield, Amp Envelope, courtesy The Showroom, photo Dan Weill Photography, p.153 Stephens House & Gardens © Abigail Willis, p.154 © Victoria Miro, p.157 © Wellcome Collection, p.158 © Zabludowicz Collection, p.161 2 Willow Road © National Trust, p.162 © Leighton House / photo Dirk Lindner, p.164 © Metro Publications, p.167

348

About us:

Based in London, Metro is a small independent publishing company with a reputation for producing well-researched and beautifully-designed guides.

London's Hidden Walks Series

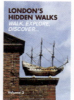

A wonderful way to explore this sometimes secretive city." Robert Elms, BBC London 94.9FM

2nd Edition

"What a great book"
Joe Swift

The
**LONDON
GARDEN
BOOK** A-Z

Abigail Willis

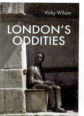

Vicky Wilson

**LONDON'S
ODDITIES**

**LONDON
ARCHITECTURE**

MARIANNE BUTLER

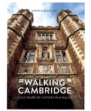

ANDREW KERSHMAN

**WALKING
CAMBRIDGE**
1,000 YEARS OF HISTORY IN 6 WALKS

ANDREW KERSHMAN

**WALKING
BRIGHTON
& HOVE**

500 YEARS OF HISTORY IN 8 WALKS

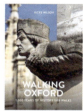

VICKY WILSON

**WALKING
OXFORD**
1,000 YEARS OF HISTORY IN 6 WALKS

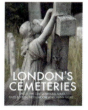

**LONDON'S
CEMETERIES**
FIND THE GRAVES OF KARL MARX,
FREDDIE MERCURY, ROGER MOORE AND MANY MORE

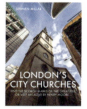

STEPHEN MILLAR

**LONDON'S
CITY CHURCHES**
FIND THE SCORCH MARKS OF THE GREAT FIRE,
OR VISIT AN ALTAR BY HENRY MOORE

EDWARD PRENDEVILLE

**VEGGIE
&VEGAN
LONDON**

**LONDON'S
HOUSES**
*FROM WORKHOUSE
TO ROYAL PALACE,
COME IN, CLOSE THE
DOOR AND STEP
BACK IN TIME...*

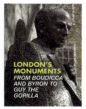

**LONDON'S
MONUMENTS**
*FROM BOUDICCA
AND BYRON TO
GUY THE
GORILLA*

**LONDON'S PARKS
AND GARDENS**
*COVER MORE
THAN TWENTY-FIVE
PERCENT OF THE
CAPITAL — THAT'S
A LOT MORE GRASS
BETWEEN TOES
THAN ANY OTHER
CITY IN EUROPE*

Hunterian Museum

Museums and Galleries of London

Written by Eve Kershman
Cover photograph Courtesy Pace Gallery, London
© Giddeon Appah, photo Damian Griffiths
Edited by Edward Prendeville
Book design by Susi Koch and Lesley Gilmour

Publisher Acknowledgement
The first edition of Museums & Galleries of London was written by
Abigail Willis and first published by Metro Publications in 1998.
Abigail went on to write a further five editions of the title for Metro
Publications and we would like to thank Abigail for her contribution to
the success of this title over 25 years of working together on it.

7th edition published in 2023 by Metro Publications Ltd
www.metropublications.com

Printed and bound in China

© 2023 Metro Publications Ltd
British Library Cataloguing in Publication Data.
A catalogue record for this book is
available from
the British Library.

ISBN 978-1-902910-74-1

MIX
Paper | Supporting
responsible forestry
FSC® C016973
www.fsc.org